REAL ESTATE Exam PREP

2nd Edition

TENNESSEE

Dearborn™
Real Estate Education

While a great deal of care has been taken to provide accurate and current information, the ideas, suggestions, general principles, and conclusions presented in this text are subject to local, state, and federal laws and regulations, court cases, and any revisions of same. The reader is urged to consult legal counsel regarding any points of law. This publication should not be used as a substitute for competent legal advice.

President: Roy Lipner
Vice President of Product Development and Publishing: Evan M. Butterfield
Development Editor: Aaron Woodrow
Director of Production: Daniel Frey
Production Editor: Caitlin Ostrow
Creative Director: Lucy Jenkins
Cover Design: Gail Chandler

Consulting Editor: Ray Bouder
Exam Prep Series Content Consultant: Marie Spodek, DREI

Introduction

Welcome to *Tennessee Exam Prep*! When you bought this book, you showed that you are serious about passing the exam and getting your real estate license. This is *NOT* an easy test. For people whose test-taking skills are weak, or who haven't adequately prepared, the exam can be a nightmare. For those who have taken the time and effort to study and review, however, the exam can be a much more positive experience.

It's pretty obvious, though, that if you practice and review key material, your test score will improve. This book is your key to exam success.

The process is simple: Just work your way through the practice questions, taking your time and answering each one carefully. Then check your answers by studying the Answer Key, where you'll find both the correct answer to each question as well as an explanation of *why* that answer is correct. It might be a good idea to review your classroom materials and textbook before you start.

Remember: These 198 questions reflect as closely as possible the topic coverage of the state-specific portion of your exam only! For the balance of the test, you'll need to use a "national" exam prep book. And remember, too, that it takes study and hard work on your part to pass the licensing exam: no single study aid will do the trick alone.

Experts who are familiar with the Tennessee licensing examination, as well as real estate law and practice, prepared this book. You've taken the first step toward your success as a real estate professional. Good Luck!

Dearborn Real Estate Education

1. In Tennessee, the real estate license law is administered by the

   1. Tennessee Human Rights Commission.
   2. Tennessee Real Estate Commission.
   3. Tennessee Association of REALTORS®.
   4. Department of Housing and Urban Development (HUD).

2. How are members of the Tennessee Real Estate Commission selected?

   1. By the governor
   2. Public election
   3. By the Tennessee Association of REALTORS®
   4. Elected by real estate licensees

3. The Tennessee Real Estate Commission has the authority to

   1. compose the examination questions on the state exam.
   2. make and enforce the rules by which all real estate licensees must abide.
   3. administer the exams given at the testing sites.
   4. enact the laws that govern real estate licensees.

4. The Tennessee Real Estate Commission may undertake an investigation of a licensee based on all the following grounds EXCEPT

   1. its own initiative.
   2. a random selection of licensees.
   3. a motion from the members of the commission.
   4. a written complaint submitted by a member of the public.

5. How many years is a commissioner's term of appointment?

   1. Three
   2. Five
   3 Six
   4. Seven

6. All of the following statements regarding the Tennessee Real Estate Commission are true EXCEPT that

   1. the commission makes and enforces the rules by which all real estate licensees must abide.
   2. the examinations that must be taken by all applicants for real estate licensing are administered by an independent testing company under the commission's direction.
   3. the state association of REALTORS® selects members of the commission.
   4. the operation of the commission's activities is administered by an executive director specifically hired for that purpose.

7. How many members serve on the Tennessee Real Estate Commission?

   1. Three
   2. Five
   3. Six
   4. Nine

8. How many of the commissioners are either licensed brokers or affiliate brokers?

   1. Three brokers and two affiliates
   2. Three brokers and three affiliates
   3. Seven members must be brokers and/or affiliate brokers
   4. All nine are brokers

9. From what grand divisions are the non-licensee members of the commission selected?

    1. Two non-licensee members are selected to serve on the commission who must be from different grand divisions.
    2. One non-licensee is selected from the North Grand Division and one is selected from the South Grand division.
    3. One non-licensee is selected from Nashville and one is selected from Memphis.
    4. Both non-licensee commissioners are selected from the central grand division, where the capitol is located.

10. How often does the Tennessee Real Estate Commission meet?

    1. Once per year for ten days
    2. Twice a year for three days
    3. Four times a year, i.e., once each quarter
    4. Once each month for up to three days per month

11. Who, other than the executive director, serves the commission?

    1. The governor
    2. The courts
    3. A legal counsel and a director of education
    4. The Appraisal Commission

12. The Tennessee Real Estate Commission is a part of the Department of

    1. Agriculture.
    2. Transportation.
    3. Commerce and Insurance.
    4. Health, Safety, and Welfare.

13. In Tennessee, who of the following would need to be a licensed real estate broker or affiliate broker?

    1. Person who manages, for the owner or broker, leased office spaces
    2. Licensed attorney acting under a power of attorney to convey real estate
    3. Resident manager or employee, who manages for the owner or broker, an apartment, duplex, or residential complex
    4. Partnership selling a building owned by the partners

14. Who of the following is required to have a real estate license?

    1. Resident manager who collects rent on behalf of a building owner
    2. Neighbor helping an owner sell his house in exchange for the seller's sewing machine
    3. Trustee appointed by a court foreclosing on a property
    4. Executor who sells a decedent's building

15. In Tennessee, a securities dealer seller who is selling real property as a security must

    1. be licensed as an affiliate broker.
    2. also be a real estate broker and have his or her securities license endorsed by the Tennessee Real Estate Commission.
    3. be approved by the Securities and Exchange Commission only.
    4. There are no special licensing requirements for real property securities dealers.

16. Under Tennessee licensing law, a partnership, association, or corporation may obtain a real estate firm license to conduct real estate brokerage business only if

    1. every member and officer actively participating in the brokerage business has a broker's license.
    2. the broker of the firm retains a current license.
    3. all papers are filed with the secretary of state.
    4. the brokerage business has paid a one-time fee to the guaranty fund.

17. A real estate license is required for all of the following activities EXCEPT

    1. managing commercial real estate.
    2. reselling a mobile home.
    3. selling real estate.
    4. collecting rent for the use of several different apartments.

18. If engaged in real estate activities, all of the following persons are subject to the real estate licensing requirements EXCEPT

    1. appraisers.
    2. attorneys at law acting as such in the disposition of a client's property.
    3. associations, partnerships, and corporations.
    4. real property securities dealers.

19. A person within a local real estate firm is responsible for the following activities: coordinating the flow of paperwork through the office, preparing forms, and hiring and supervising clerical personnel. This person is

    1. violating the license law.
    2. required to have a broker's license.
    3. required to have an affiliate broker's license.
    4. exempt from real estate licensing requirements.

20. In Tennessee, applications for any real estate license must

    1. be completed within six months after taking and passing the state written exam.
    2. include MLS dues.
    3. be made before May 31 of each year.
    4. include letters of recommendation from three property owners.

21. In Tennessee, all of the following are requirements for obtaining a broker's license EXCEPT

    1. having successfully completed 120 hours of approved real estate courses.
    2. being at least 18 years of age.
    3. having been actively engaged as a licensed affiliate broker for at least four years.
    4. being of good moral character.

22. A person successfully completed her real estate education requirements and passed the state exam on January 15, 2005. What is the latest date on which she may apply for an affiliate broker's license?

    1. December 31, 2005
    2. July 15, 2005
    3. October 31, 2005
    4. November 1, 2005

23. Three weeks before N begins his real estate prelicense class, he offers to help his neighbor sell her house. The neighbor agrees to pay N a 5 percent commission. An offer is accepted while N is taking the class and closes the day before N passes the examination and receives his affiliate broker's license. The neighbor refuses to pay N the agreed commission. Can N sue to recover payment?

1. Yes; N was formally enrolled in a course of study intended to result in a real estate license at the time an offer was procured and accepted, and therefore the commission agreement is binding.
2. No; in Tennessee, a real estate affiliate broker must have a permanent office in which his or her license is displayed at the time of closing in order to collect a commission from a seller.
3. Yes; while the statute of frauds forbids recovery on an oral agreement for the conveyance of real property, Tennessee law permits enforcement of an oral commission contract under these facts.
4. No; state law prohibits lawsuits to collect commissions unless the injured party is a licensed broker and the license was in effect before the agreement was reached.

24. Which of the following persons must have a real estate broker's license in order to transact business?

1. Owner of a six-unit apartment building who personally manages the building, collects rents, and shows the apartments to prospective tenants
2. Person who negotiates the sales of entire businesses, including their stock equipment and buildings, for a promised fee
3. Superintendent of a large apartment building who shows apartments to prospective tenants as part of his or her regular duties
4. Son who has his parent's recorded power of attorney to negotiate the sale of the parent's residence

25. An applicant for a real estate license in Tennessee must

1. have completed at least two years of college.
2. be at least 21 years old.
3. request a hearing before the commission if he or she has a prior criminal record other than driving offenses.
4. show proof of passing the license examination any time up to ten months prior to the application.

26. Of the following, who must obtain a real estate license and is not exempt from the provisions of the Tennessee Real Estate License Act?

1. Property owner who sells or leases his or her own property
2. Individual who receives compensation for procuring prospective buyers or renters of real estate
3. Individual who is employed as a resident property manager
4. Trustee acting under a court order

27. An individual wants to sell her own house. Which of the following statements is true?

    1. She does not need a real estate license to sell her house herself.
    2. In Tennessee, anyone who sells any real property must have a real estate license issued by the real estate commission.
    3. She may obtain a temporary real estate license to legally sell her house.
    4. She may sell her house without obtaining a real estate license only if she is a licensed attorney.

28. The requirements to obtain a real estate affiliate broker's license in Tennessee include

    1. an associate degree or certificate in real estate from an accredited college, university, or proprietary school.
    2. United States citizenship and a driver's license.
    3. successful completion of 12 credit hours of real estate law, investments, finance, and appraisal.
    4. successful completion of a 60-hour course in the general principles of real estate and the 30-hour New Affiliate's course; passage of the state exam; purchase of errors and omissions insurance; and being sponsored by a licensed broker.

29. All affiliate broker real estate licenses in Tennessee are issued

    1. by the real estate school upon completion of the course.
    2. by the state licensing bureau.
    3. by the Tennessee Real Estate Commission.
    4. after one year of apprenticeship.

30. As of July 1, 2005, what is the expiration date of each broker's license in Tennessee?

    1. January 31 of every even-numbered year
    2. December 31 of each even-numbered year
    3. October 31 of each odd-numbered year
    4. 24 months from the date of license issuance

31. In order to take the broker's license exam in Tennessee, a candidate must be at least 18 years of age and

    1. show proof of closing 50 sales within the past two years, pass the broker exam, and be recommended by the firm's broker.
    2. have held an active affiliate broker's license for at least three years, complete 120 hours of approved education (30 hours of which must be the broker office management course) and receive permission from the commission to take the exam.
    3. hold a college degree in management and audit a basic principles course prior to testing.
    4. hold a master's degree or higher and audit a basic principles course prior to testing.

32. An unlicensed individual who engages in activities that require a real estate license is subject to which of the following penalties?

    1. Fine not to exceed $1,000
    2. Fine not to exceed $1,000 and one-year imprisonment
    3. Civil penalty of up to $1,000 per day for each separate violation in addition to other penalties provided by law
    4. Civil penalty not to exceed $5,000 and a mandatory prison term not to exceed five years

33. An applicant receives her real estate license in July of 2005. She has never been licensed before. How many continuing education hours must she take prior to renewing her license?

    1. 16 hours, four of which must be the Core Course
    2. 15 hours
    3. None
    4. 30 hours

34. An affiliate broker renewed his license two years ago. Now, in order to renew a second time, the affiliate broker must

    1. pay a fee of $225 only.
    2. be actively participating in the real estate business.
    3. have completed six hours of continuing education in the last two years, three hours in real estate law and three hours in fair housing.
    4. have completed 16 hours of education: the current four-hour Core Course and 12 additional hours of continuing education in the current two-year license period to renew for the next two-year license period.

35. A licensee who allows his or her license to expire has how long to reinstate the license without monetary penalty?

    1. There is no "free" time
    2. Up to 30 days
    3. No more than 365 days
    4. One year from the last June 23rd

36. In Tennessee, when do real estate licenses and errors and omissions insurance expire?

    1. Annually, in the month issued
    2. Every two years in the month of the licensee's birthday
    3. On June 30 of each even-numbered year
    4. Errors and omissions insurance expires on the last day of each even-numbered year. Starting July 1, 2005, licenses expire two years from the date of issuance.

37. After the first issuance of an affiliate broker's license, what mandatory class is required during the first year?

    1. Within one year of the exact date of issuance, a licensee must complete a first year 30-hour course.
    2. 18 hours of home study
    3. Three 12-hour classes for listing, buying, and ethics
    4. There are no mandatory requirements.

38. With respect to a nonresident license, the commission, in its discretion, may do all of the following EXCEPT

    1. refuse to issue a license.
    2. refuse to renew a license.
    3. refuse to reinstate a license.
    4. require a nonresident licensee to move to Tennessee.

39. When calling another real estate company to show one of their properties to your buyer client, what information must you disclose to the listing agent on first contact?

    1. The qualifications of the buyer.
    2. Your name, company name, and your representational status.
    3. The maximum the buyer can afford to pay.
    4. The minimum amount of commission your company will accept as a commission.

40. Which of the following may an unlicensed assistant perform under the Tennessee license law?

    1. Arguing the merits of an offer on behalf of a prospective buyer
    2. Helping prospective buyers determine an appropriate price range and geographical location for their home search
    3. Responding to general questions about the price and location of a specific property as limited by the broker
    4. Assisting a buyer through the closing process

41. Routine services that do not create an agency or broker relationship are referred to as

    1. transactional acts.
    2. routine brokerage.
    3. ministerial acts.
    4. customer service.

42. In Tennessee, an unlicensed real estate assistant may perform all of the following activities EXCEPT

    1. compute commission checks.
    2. assemble legal documents required for a closing.
    3. explain simple contract documents to prospective buyers.
    4. prepare and distribute flyers and promotional materials for approval by the licensee and the broker.

43. Personal real estate assistants in Tennessee

    1. must be licensed.
    2. may insert factual information into contract forms under the employing broker's supervision and approval.
    3. may independently host open houses and home show booths.
    4. must be unlicensed individuals.

44. A broker's unlicensed assistant worked late nights and weekends to help ensure the successful closing of a difficult transaction. The assistant's extra work included making several phone calls to the prospective buyers, encouraging them to accept the seller's counteroffer. Largely because of the assistant's efforts, the sale went through with no problem. Now the broker wants to pay the assistant a percentage of the commission, "because the assistant has really earned it." Under Tennessee law, the broker may

1. compensate the assistant in the form of a commission under the circumstances described here.
2. not pay the assistant a cash commission but is permitted to make a gift of tangible personal property.
3. not compensate the assistant for assisting in the negotiations. The broker and the assistant are both in violation of rules regarding unlicensed assistants.
4. pay a commission to the assistant only if the assistant is an independent contractor.

45. An affiliate broker with XYZ Realty has scheduled to hold an open house on one of his listings this coming Saturday. On Friday, he learns he must go out of town and needs to find someone else to hold his open house in his place. Which of the following is true?

1. His unlicensed wife can do it for him so long as he does not pay her on a commission basis.
2. His unlicensed assistant may hold the open house as part of her regular duties without special compensation.
3. If he cannot find another licensee in his own company, he may compensate another licensed agent from another realty company to hold the open house.
4. Only another licensed agent within XYZ Realty may hold the open house for this affiliate broker.

46. An unlicensed real estate assistant may

1. host open houses for affiliate brokers.
2. host booths at fairs.
3. unlock a property for a customer under the direction of the agent.
4. negotiate the terms of a lease.

47. A licensee's unlicensed assistant may not

1. prepare a market analysis.
2. gather tax assessor's information for the affiliate broker.
3. prepare an advertisement for the approval of the licensee and the broker.
4. act as a go-between with the buyer and seller for the affiliate broker.

48. An unlicensed assistant may do all of the following EXCEPT

1. compute the amount of a commission check for the broker.
2. keep notes of training sessions for the broker.
3. make cold calls for the affiliate broker.
4. be paid on an hourly basis.

49. An unlicensed assistant may not

1. be paid on the basis of the employing licensee's real estate activity.
2. accept security deposits on apartments for the owner or managing broker.
3. allow tenants to sign a lease.
4. order repairs on properties for the licensee.

50. A part-time unlicensed assistant works for an affiliate broker. The assistant wrote three ads for the affiliate and placed them in a local paper. Which of the following is true?

1. This is standard clerical work and is permitted by the Tennessee Real Estate Broker Act.
2. The assistant must have the ads approved by the affiliate broker only before placing them in the local paper.
3. The affiliate broker and his managing broker must approve the ads prior to being placed in a local paper.
4. The assistant is not permitted to write ads unless he or she is licensed.

51. Two licensed affiliate brokers, M and J, work for XYZ Realty. M gave J $100 for holding an open house for him last Saturday. In this situation,

1. M followed Tennessee license laws by hiring a licensed assistant within his own company.
2. J complied with the Tennessee license laws by only working for another agent within the same company.
3. their actions were proper, so long as their broker was aware of the event.
4. both M and J were in violation of the law.

52. Licensed real estate assistants may

1. be paid directly by the affiliate broker for whom they work.
2. delay paying taxes on work performed for affiliates through Rule 74.
3. work for a broker of another firm if paid on an hourly basis when showing an open house for that broker.
4. be paid on a commission basis by the broker of the firm for work performed for other agents within the same firm if the work requires a license.

53. If a person obtains a Tennessee reciprocal (nonresident) real estate license, he or she must

1. be licensed as a broker or affiliate broker in any state.
2. establish a principal place of business in Tennessee or be licensed under a resident Tennessee broker.
3. file an irrevocable consent agreement with the commission.
4. take all education course requirements in the state of Tennessee.

54. What must a nonresident license applicant file with the commission?

1. A certificate of specific performance
2. An irrevocable consent to suit
3. A corpus delicti
4. A copy of their birth certificate

55. A broker received a buyer's earnest money check for $5,000 and immediately cashed it. At closing, the broker handed the seller a personal check drawn on the broker's own bank account for $5,300, representing the original earnest money plus six percent interest. The broker

    1. should have deposited the money in the broker's business account.
    2. should have deposited the money in the broker's escrow or trust account.
    3. properly cashed the check, but should have kept the interest.
    4. should have deposited the money in his personal bank account, and would have been entitled to keep the interest as a service fee.

56. A broker has obtained an offer to purchase a residence that is listed with his firm. After the buyers sign a purchase and sale agreement and the broker accepts their earnest money deposit, the broker must

    1. deposit the earnest money in the broker's personal checking account for safekeeping until closing.
    2. complete a second earnest money/sales agreement form that states an exaggerated selling price and give the second form to the buyers to present to the lender so that they will be certain to obtain sufficient financing for their purchase.
    3. immediately provide a copy of the agreement and a receipt for the deposit to the buyers.
    4. file the agreement in the broker's records and, when two or three other offers have been received for the property, present them all to the sellers, who then may choose the best offer.

57. The on-site property manager for Acme Apartments is responsible for negotiating leases for the apartments. In this position, the on-site manager

    1. is exempt from the license laws.
    2. must have a broker's license.
    3. must have an affiliate broker's or broker's license.
    4. is violating the license law.

58. State law requires that a preprinted offer to purchase that is intended to become a binding contract have which of the following headings?

    1. No particular heading on a contract is required by law in Tennessee
    2. Offer to Purchase
    3. Standard Purchase Offer and Contract
    4. Purchase Offer Form

59. A broker wants to list a property but is getting a lot of competition from other brokers who would also like to list it. The broker offers the seller the following inducement to sign his listing agreement: "I'll buy your property if it doesn't sell in 90 days." With this inducement, the broker must do all of the following EXCEPT

    1. buy the property at the agreed upon figure at any time during the 90 days.
    2. market the property as if no special agreement existed.
    3. show the seller evidence of the broker's financial ability to buy the property.
    4. show the seller written details of the plan before any contract of guaranty is signed.

60. Which of the following agreements must be in writing?

    1. Closed listing
    2. Open listing for less than a year
    3. Exclusive-right-to-sell agency
    4. Net listing

61. In Tennessee, the age of legal competence is

    1. 18.
    2. 19.
    3. 20.
    4. 21.

62. Broker M shows Broker J's listing. Along with an offer to purchase, Broker M receives $2,000 earnest money from a buyer. Broker M retains the earnest money with Broker J's permission and leaves the country, never to be heard from again. The buyers complain to the real estate commission and show the receipt that Broker M gave them for the earnest money. Who is responsible for the earnest money if broker M cannot be found?

    1. E&O insurance company
    2. Education and recovery account
    3. Broker J
    4. Seller

63. When disbursing funds from an escrow account, the broker should

    1. pay them to his or her operating account and then disburse them to the person conducting the closing.
    2. pay them to the buyer just before closing.
    3. pay them to the mortgage lender at closing.
    4. disburse the funds in a proper manner without unreasonable delay.

64. Where a contract authorizes a broker to place funds in an escrow or trustee account, the broker must clearly specify in the contract

    1. that the buyer will default if the contract is not closed on time.
    2. that the seller has the power to declare the buyer in default if the buyer does not perform.
    3. the name and address of the person who will actually hold the funds and the terms and conditions for disbursement of the funds.
    4. the name of the affiliate broker who holds the earnest money.

65. If a broker acts as the closing agent, the broker must provide each customer or client a copy of the

    1. listing agreement.
    2. property survey.
    3. abstract of title.
    4. closing documents.

66. Which of the following situations would satisfy the two-year CE requirement in Tennessee?

    1. 12-hour course on using real estate office spreadsheet programs, offered by a local community college
    2. 6-hour course on managing agricultural property, offered by an approved CE sponsor
    3. Retaking and passing the licensing exam and applying for a new license
    4. Teaching a prelicensing course several evenings a week

67. A broker who holds a Tennessee license by reciprocity, but whose state of residence is Mississippi, will be exempt from the requirement that he or she maintain a definite place of business in Tennessee if all of the following factors are met EXCEPT

    1. maintaining an office in Mississippi.
    2. maintaining an active broker's license in the state of Mississippi.
    3. employing at least one Tennessee licensee.
    4. filing a written statement appointing the commissioner as his or her Tennessee agent for service of process, submitting to the Tennessee Real Estate Commission's jurisdiction, and agreeing to abide by the provisions of the license act.

68. A person must be licensed as a real estate broker or affiliate broker if that person is

    1. selling his or her house.
    2. buying a house for his or her personal use.
    3. engaging in the real estate brokerage business.
    4. constructing houses.

69. Who, other than the real estate commission, can revoke a real estate license?

    1. Governor
    2. Board or association of REALTORS®
    3. Court of competent jurisdiction
    4. Broker of the firm

70. Mark holds a nonresident real estate affiliate broker license in Mississippi. Mark's home state has reciprocity with Mississippi, but does not have reciprocity with Tennessee. Can Mark obtain a Tennessee nonresident affiliate broker's license?

    1. Yes, if Mark can find a Tennessee broker to sponsor him
    2. No, because it is illegal to have a nonresident license in more than one state
    3. Yes, because Mississippi has reciprocity with Tennessee
    4. No, because Mark's state of residence does not have reciprocity with Tennessee

71. The application fee for an affiliate broker or broker's license is

    1. $60.
    2. $100.
    3. $125.
    4. $195.

72. If a court revokes a broker's or affiliate broker's license, how may it be reissued?

    1. By completing a 30-hour penalty course, paying a $100 reinstatement fee, and passing the license examination administered by ASI
    2. Through an appeal to the governor via the local state representative
    3. By petitioning the Tennessee Association of REALTORS®
    4. Upon the consenting vote of six of the members of the commission

73. A broker will have held a broker's license for three years by the end of next week. She realizes she will not be able to complete her 120 hours of post-licensing education in the remaining time. How will she be able to continue to legally sell other people's real estate for a fee?

    1. She cannot sell after next week; her license will automatically be revoked.
    2. She will have to work for referral fees only until her license expires.
    3. She may request an extension of up to one year and pay a fee of $100.
    4. While her license is still valid, she is entitled to request, in writing, to surrender her broker's license for an affiliate broker's license.

74. After passing the affiliate broker examination, P found a sponsoring broker and mailed his license application, signed by the broker, to the commission with all the necessary monies and paperwork. The next day, a neighbor expressed a desire to let P list his property "for sale." P was afraid that if he waited until the license was issued, the neighbor might list the property for sale with another agent. P's broker, after checking with P's real estate school instructor, told him that because he was almost licensed, it would be permissible to list the property because P would have his license by the time a commission was received. That same day, P, as a subagent of his broker, listed the property for sale. All of the following are true EXCEPT that

    1. because P would be licensed by the time the property sale closed, and no commission was paid prior to his being licensed, P and his broker acted in accordance with the license laws.
    2. because P's license was not issued at the time he listed the property for sale, P was performing an illegal act.
    3. because P's license was not issued at the time he listed the property for sale, his broker had no authority to let him list the property.
    4. P could be subject to a fine and imprisonment.

75. The broker of XYZ Realty has an affiliate broker with 18 years of experience. May the affiliate broker be appointed as manager of the firm?

    1. Yes, with at least five years of experience, the affiliate broker should be well qualified to manage the other licensees.
    2. No, an affiliate broker may not manage a real estate office regardless of how many years of experience he or she may have.
    3. No, an affiliate broker must also be the owner of the firm to manage it.
    4. Yes, a real estate office may be managed by anyone.

76. How many miles away from the firm's office may an affiliate broker sell real estate?

    1. 50 miles
    2. Within a 100-mile radius
    3. Within the same county
    4. Distance is not specified by law

77. How many miles away from the firm's office may an affiliate broker reside?

    1. Up to 50 miles without a waiver from the Commission
    2. Within a 100-mile radius
    3. Within the same county
    4. The law does not specify the distance

78. An affiliate broker works for a managing broker who normally works from 9:00 A.M. to 4:00 P.M. managing a grocery store. The broker

    1. needs to stay in contact with the affiliate broker several times a week.
    2. will supervise the affiliate's progress during the broker's off-hours from the grocery store.
    3. will permit the affiliate broker to write necessary earnest money checks for closings.
    4. cannot hire an affiliate broker without being available to the affiliate broker at some time each day, and then only with a waiver from the Commission.

79. A licensee with five active listings is planning to leave his current broker to work for another broker. In the meantime, the licensee had two closings yesterday, and his broker has informed him that she is keeping those commission checks because he has not paid for several advertising bills that he earlier charged to her company. The licensee is upset and calls the commission to ask if he should file a complaint against his broker or if the commission will resolve this dispute. In this situation, the commission will advise the licensee

    1. to put his complaint in writing and forward it to them for resolution.
    2. to complain to the Better Business Bureau.
    3. to sue his broker for the commission and to take his other five listings to his new broker next week.
    4. that the commission does not handle commission disputes.

80. A licensee with six active listings is planning to leave his current broker to work for another broker. The broker tells the licensee that he may not take any of the six unsold listings to his next firm. In this situation, the licensee

    1. should contact the owners of the five property listings he obtained and ask them to direct the broker to assign the listings to his new broker.
    2. should sue the broker to make her let him take the listings to his new broker's firm.
    3. may not take the listings since the listings are with the broker, not the affiliate.
    4. does not need his broker's permission to take the listings with him to the new broker because the licensee had obtained the listings.

81. A person successfully passed her broker's exam and has applied for her broker's license and firm license. She plans to operate her company out of her home to save money. Her home is in a residential subdivision of over 2,000 houses and the subdivision would be an ideal location to farm for listings. This applicant

    1. will not be issued a license.
    2. should have picked a smaller subdivision to be successful.
    3. has chosen a subdivision that is just the right size.
    4. may not be successful unless she hires more agents.

82. A broker found a home in an area that was just rezoned for commercial business. The broker leased the home, moved into it, and used it for a real estate office. The broker hired three agents and advised them to do a lot of advertising because the broker did not have or want a sign outside the broker's home. In this situation, the broker

    1. and the agents may operate out of this house because it is in a commercial place of business in full compliance with the license rules.
    2. does not need a sign outside the house.
    3. must use letters at least four inches high if the broker installs a sign.
    4. is violating commission rules by the lack of a sign outside of the office/home.

83. In a real estate transaction, a broker's commission

    1. is determined according to the standard rates set by agreement of local real estate brokers.
    2. must be stated in the listing agreement and is negotiated between the broker and seller.
    3. is determined through arbitration by the Tennessee Real Estate Commission, but only if there is a dispute.
    4. must be paid with cash or a cashier's check upon closing.

84. A seller told an affiliate broker, "I don't care how much you get for my farm. All I want is $250,000. You may keep all you get over that amount." The affiliate listed the property as directed by the seller. The farm sold for $450,000 and the affiliate broker kept $200,000 as commission. All of the following are true EXCEPT that

    1. the affiliate broker was not working in the best interests of the seller.
    2. the seller received the net amount he wanted; however, the listing was illegal.
    3. because the seller received the net amount he asked for, the affiliate's commission was acceptable and everything was above board and legal.
    4. the listing that does not include the price excluding the customary commission and expenses associated with the sale is illegal in Tennessee.

85. An affiliate broker received an offer from an agent in another firm. The listing was obtained by the affiliate for his broker. The affiliate broker is scheduled to show the same listed property tomorrow, so he wants to hold the offer until the next day so he might be able to take the two offers to the seller. In this situation, the affiliate broker

    1. is working in the seller's best interests by waiting a day to present the offer because the seller can accept the better of the two offers.
    2. must promptly present the other agent's offer.
    3. should not accept an offer from another agent knowing that the property was going to be shown the next day.
    4. should call the seller and advise the seller that the affiliate will be presenting one or possibly two offers the next day.

86. An affiliate broker presented an offer to his principal, the seller. The seller decided to hold on to the offer to consider it. Later that day, the affiliate received two more offers on the same property: one in writing and the other a verbal offer. What must the affiliate do?

    1. Present all written offers to the seller until the seller has accepted one of them
    2. Tell the seller about both offers and advise him he must accept or reject the first offer before he will deliver the written offer for his consideration
    3. Advise the seller that the verbal offer is better because it is for more money than the other two written offers
    4. Return the second written offer to the prospective buyer advising that there is a contract pending

87. A broker overheard the seller tell the buyer that he would leave the drapes with the house. Since drapes are personal property and not real property, the broker did not include the drapes in the offer to purchase. The broker knew the seller was honest and would leave the drapes with the house. Which of the following is true?

    1. Drapes are personal property and therefore need not be included in the real estate contract. The seller is bound by his word.
    2. Because drapes are personal property and not real property, they cannot be included in the sale.
    3. The broker wrote the offer as in a proper manner.
    4. The broker has committed an error of omission.

88. The affiliate broker, in an attempt to persuade a seller to list his property for sale with him, made several promises. In this situation, the agent

    1. has not violated the license laws by attempting to influence the seller to do business with his firm.
    2. is not permitted to make promises; this is one of the 21 ways to lose your license.
    3. should not attempt to induce the seller to enter any contract based on promises made by the agent.
    4. may find that the seller has rightfully complained to the commission about the agent's actions.

89. A seller and his agent agreed not to tell a prospective buyer about the leaking roof on the house. Because the buyer did not specifically ask about the condition of the roof, the agent did not mention the subject when he showed him the property. Which of the following is true?

    1. The long-standing rule of *caveat emptor* (let the buyer beware) holds that there is no obligation to inform the buyer if he does not ask. Therefore there is no need to tell the buyer about the leaking roof.
    2. To disclose this confidential information, the agent would violate his fiduciary relationship with his client, the seller.
    3. The seller should sue the agent if he discloses this information.
    4. The agent must disclose this information to the prospective buyer.

90. A new affiliate broker is eager to list a business for sale. The business owner belongs to the American Businesswoman's Organization. In an attempt to get the listing, the affiliate broker tells the business owner that she also belongs to that organization, when in fact she does not. The affiliate also states that she is a REALTOR®, when in fact she has not yet joined the association. Which of the following statements are true?

    1. The commission may revoke the affiliate broker's license.
    2. The affiliate broker, while telling a few lies about what organizations she belongs to, did not say anything that would affect the listing itself, and therefore did not injure the business owner.
    3. Since the affiliate broker's comments were trivial, there will be no consequences as the commission does not handle minor details such as this.
    4. The affiliate broker will automatically lose her license.

91. An affiliate broker received an earnest money check from the buyer with the initial offer to purchase. He took the offer to the listing agency for acceptance. The offer has been countered three times in the last five days. So as not to cause confusion, the affiliate has the check paper-clipped to the offer, as evidence to show each party the earnest money exists. The affiliate broker signed on the offer for receipt of the check and gave the buyer a copy of the offer upon receipt. In this situation, the affiliate broker

    1. has acted in accordance with proper business procedures and the license laws.
    2. should have made a copy of the check.
    3. should have put the check in the office listing folder file drawer with a copy of the offer.
    4. failed to safeguard and immediately remit funds coming into his possession.

92. Purchasers who were being shown a dental clinic for sale said they wanted to write up an offer immediately. The broker pulled a contract form from his briefcase and filled it out. The purchasers signed it, giving the broker $5,000 earnest money, and received a receipt for the money. The broker and the purchasers departed and the broker then had copies made of the offer. An hour later, the broker delivered a copy to the purchasers. As the purchasers studied the offer more carefully that evening, they were shocked by some of the obligations to which they were committed. They suspected that the broker changed some of the wording in the offer before giving them their copy. They contacted the commission and complained. The commission will tell the purchasers

1. that they do not interfere with contract negotiations.
2. that they should have received a copy immediately upon signing the offer, and that they could file a complaint to the commission.
3. that they should have read the offer more carefully.
4. to call the board of REALTORS®.

93. A purchaser instructed the seller's agent to put in the offer that the closing date was "to be agreed upon." The seller accepted the offer. Later, the purchaser and the seller could never agree on the closing date. The purchaser wanted his earnest money refunded and the seller declared him in default. Which of the following is correct?

1. The seller was right; the purchaser had an obligation to agree on a closing date and since he did not agree, he was in default.
2. The purchaser was right and should get his money back because the seller was unreasonable and would not agree on a closing date.
3. They are both wrong because they should have come to an agreement as stated in the offer. The seller owes the affiliate broker's broker a full commission for finding a ready, willing, and able buyer. It is not the agent's fault they could not agree when they were bound to do so.
4. The affiliate broker is at fault because he failed to require a definite termination date in the sales contract.

94. A buyer prospect told the seller's listing agent that she would like to purchase the house she was just shown, but she still had six months to go on her lease. The listing agent said, "Bring me that lease. I'll show you how to get out of it and how to buy this house." If the agent is successful, which of the following is true?

1. The agent can lose his or her license and also be charged with practicing law without a license.
2. One of the best things an agent can do for a customer is to get him or her out of an apartment and into a home of his or her own. The agent has earned his or her commission.
3. The agent will never regret helping her get into her own home and start building an equity.
4. The agent's broker should be happy with the agent's performance.

95. An Asian couple came into the broker's office and expressed a desire to purchase a home. The helpful broker only showed them homes in a predominantly Asian area of town so that they would feel more comfortable in their surroundings. Did the broker do anything wrong?

1. Yes, he is guilty of blockbusting.
2. Yes, he is guilty of racial steering.
3. Yes, he is guilty of redlining.
4. No, people are more comfortable living near people of their own ethnicity.

96. A broker welcomed a new affiliate to the firm, saying "We're so happy to have you as a member of our team. Go get 'em, tiger." That was the entire training session for the affiliate. Later, the affiliate committed several errors of omission in writing an offer, which was preceded by showing the buyers another company's listing in which the affiliate had failed to obtain permission to show the property. The sellers were upset and complained to the commission. Under these circumstances, the broker

1. did nothing wrong; the affiliate passed the real estate course and met the state's standards by passing the state affiliate broker's license exam. If anything, the state should have a better test.
2. cannot be charged with anything. The broker has many agents and cannot be with all of them at the same time to ensure they do everything right.
3. should have had a more intensive interview with affiliate.
4. failed to exercise adequate supervision over the activities of his affiliates.

97. Broker G recommended that his seller contact Contractor C to repair several loose boards on the back porch of the house he just listed. The contractor sent the broker a check for the referral. Broker B did not disclose to the seller that he would receive a referral from Contractor C. Which of the following statements is true?

    1. This referral is a standard real estate practice.
    2. The broker need not tell the seller about receiving the referral.
    3. The acceptance of an undisclosed fee, commission, or rebate (that the seller paid the repair people) can result in a loss of license.
    4. The affiliate was only doing his job by helping the seller prepare his house for sale. The referral fee was just incidental.

98. A well-known broker in town listed a local store for sale and now wants to purchase it. To keep the price from becoming inflated, he had a neighbor contract to purchase it and assign the contract to him as soon as the seller accepted the offer. After the closing, the seller complained to the commission that he was unaware that the purchaser was his broker, and accused him of an unethical act. What can the commission do about this situation?

    1. Nothing. A real estate broker has the same rights as anyone in purchasing property. There was no duty to tell the seller of the broker's intentions.
    2. The commission can rescind the sale and let the seller put it back on the market.
    3. The commission can require the broker to pay damages to the seller.
    4. The commission can suspend or revoke the broker's license for failing to disclose to the owner his intention or true position when offering to purchase a property listed with his office.

99. A broker has obtained an offer to purchase a residence that is listed with his firm. After the buyers sign a purchase and sale agreement, and the broker receives the earnest money, the broker must

1. deposit the earnest money in the broker's personal checking account for safekeeping until closing.
2. complete a second earnest money/sales agreement form that states an exaggerated selling price and give the second form to the buyers to present to the lender so that they will be certain to obtain sufficient financing for their purchase.
3. immediately provide a copy of the agreement and a receipt for deposit to the buyers.
4. file the agreement in the broker's records and, when two or three other offers have been received for the property, present them all to the sellers, who then may choose the best offer.

100. In Tennessee, which of the following is legal and will not result in license revocation?

1. Being convicted of a felony in Tennessee or any other state
2. Advertising in a newspaper that he or she is a member of the Tennessee Association of REALTORS® when in fact he or she is not
3. Depositing escrow money in his or her personal checking account
4. Agreeing with a seller to accept a listing for more than the normal commission rate

101. The commission has the power to revoke an affiliate broker's license if the affiliate broker

1. attempts to have her company represent another real estate company through subagency after obtaining her broker's consent.
2. attempts to represent a buyer.
3. enters into an exclusive-listing contract.
4. deposits a buyer's down payment in her own personal or operating bank account.

102. In Tennessee, a broker may have his or her license suspended or revoked for all of the following actions EXCEPT

1. being declared mentally incompetent.
2. depositing earnest money into the firm's escrow account.
3. helping another person cheat on the licensing examination.
4. displaying a "For Sale" sign on a property without the owner's consent.

103. For which of the following acts may the real estate commission suspend or revoke a licensee's license?

1. Making promises
2. Having been found liable in a civil trial of illegal discrimination
3. Offering gifts or prizes
4. Failing to provide information requested by a bank within 30 days of the request

104. Which of the following actions is legal and not a violation of license law?

    1. Encouraging a seller to reject an offer because the prospective buyer is a Methodist
    2. Placing a "For Sale" sign in front of a house after receiving the seller's written permission to do so
    3. Advertising that individuals who attend a promotional presentation will receive a prize without mentioning that they will also have to take a day trip to a new subdivision site
    4. Encouraging a buyer to deal with you because you are a REALTOR®, when in fact you are not

105. If a broker tells a lender that the sales price stated on the sales contract is higher than the original listed price,

    1. the buyer must always pay the difference in cash.
    2. the buyer is likely to receive an interest rate break.
    3. the broker can lose his or her license and be fined and/or imprisoned.
    4. the buyer can receive a higher mortgage amount if an appraisal reflects the higher amount.

106. Janet X, an affiliate broker, paid the telephone company to list her name in the directory under the real estate heading as "Janet X, Real Estate Affiliate Broker, Residential Property My Specialty." Based on this information, Janet must also include

    1. her license number.
    2. the expiration date of her license.
    3. her street address.
    4. the firm's name and the firm's telephone number.

107. A broker who wishes to place a "For Sale" sign on a listed property must first

    1. obtain the written consent of the owner of the property.
    2. sell the property.
    3. show the property.
    4. get permission from the neighbors.

108. When advertising real property for sale, real estate licensees

    1. may state only the licensee's box number or street address.
    2. may simply give a telephone number to call for more information.
    3. must include the firm's name and the firm's telephone number in the advertisement.
    4. must identify the owner of the property.

109. A real estate affiliate broker decides to sell his own property without listing the property with his broker. When advertising the property, the affiliate broker

    1. must disclose the name, address, and phone number of his employing broker.
    2. must disclose the fact that he owns the property free and clear of all loans.
    3. must include the designation "owner/agent" in all ads, if acting as a private citizen.
    4. is prohibited from selling his own home in this manner by license law.

110. A broker had developed a Web site advertising properties listed with his office. What, if anything, must the broker include in the advertisement?

    1. The company name and telephone number
    2. The firm's real estate license number
    3. The address of each property listed in the advertisement
    4. The firm's address

111. An affiliate broker has developed an Internet Web site. What, if anything, must the affiliate broker include?

    1. Name and telephone number of the office that holds the affiliate broker's license on every page of the Web site
    2. Name of the home office of the company that holds the affiliate broker's license and a list of states in which the company is licensed
    3. Names of all licensees in the broker's office and a list of states in which they are licensed
    4. There is no need for any particular disclosures

112. In a real estate transaction, a broker's commission

    1. must be stated in the listing agreement and is negotiated between the broker and seller.
    2. is determined according to the standard rates set by agreement of local real estate brokers.
    3. will be determined through arbitration by the Tennessee Real Estate Commission if the parties cannot agree.
    4. must be paid with cash or a cashier's check upon closing.

113. Broker M ran an advertisement suggesting that buyers deal directly with him instead of working with "pushy agents." Because of this ad, the broker

    1. may be punished by the commission for running an improper ad in making disparaging remarks about fellow licensees.
    2. may say whatever he wants to in the ad since he is the broker.
    3. must identify those "pushy agents" by name in his ad.
    4. must have the commission approve any ad prior to publication.

114. An affiliate broker owns two rental properties. He does not want to list them through his or any real estate firm. When advertising them for rent, the affiliate

    1. has the same rights as any citizen and does not need to have any special wording in the ad, so long as they are not listed with a company.
    2. must list them for rent through his broker's company and pay the normal commission.
    3. may not require a security deposit of the tenant.
    4. must include the term "owner/agent" in any sign or other ad.

115. Listings based on a "net price" are

    1. more profitable because no minimum is set on the amount of commission collectable.
    2. legal in Tennessee as long as the seller agrees.
    3. illegal in Tennessee at any time.
    4. permissible with approval of the real estate commission.

116. A church owns six rental houses. They will only rent them to members of the same religion. Their action is

    1. in violation of the Americans with Disabilities Act.
    2. in violation of the Civil Rights Act.
    3. not in violation of human rights so long as they do not discriminate in their selection of members.
    4. in violation of the Federal Fair Housing Act.

117. Commissions earned by a broker in a real estate sales transaction

    1. are determined by agreement of the broker and his or her principal.
    2. may be shared with an unlicensed person, provided that such person aided the broker in bringing the buyer and seller together.
    3. may be deducted from the earnest money deposit and claimed by the broker as soon as the buyer and seller execute the purchase and sale agreement.
    4. are based on a schedule of commission rates set by the Tennessee Real Estate Commission.

118. All funds received by a broker on behalf of his or her principal must be deposited in an escrow or trust account

    1. three days after receiving the offer.
    2. within three days of obtaining all signatures for the contract.
    3. no later than five working days after receiving the offer.
    4. promptly upon the acceptance of the offer unless specifically directed otherwise by the contract.

119. When should an affiliate broker pay his or her broker the earnest money?

    1. Within three business days of receipt of the funds
    2. Immediately upon receipt
    3. The earnest money stays with the offer and counteroffers until it becomes a binding contract, at which time it is given to the listing firm
    4. Hold the earnest money deposit in the listing folder in the broker's real estate brokerage office until the offer is accepted

120. An affiliate broker received an offer and a $5,000 earnest money check from her buyer. She paper-clipped the check to the offer and submitted the offer to the listing agent. One day later, the listing agent returned a counteroffer and the check. The buyer accepted the seller's counteroffer. The acceptance and check were returned to the listing agent, who presented the check to her broker for deposit to the broker's escrow account. Did the agents act properly?

    1. Yes; both acted in a professional manner.
    2. No; the buyer's agent should have retained the check.
    3. No; affiliate brokers are required to deliver the earnest money to their broker immediately upon receipt.
    4. Yes; as long as there are counteroffers, the check may accompany the document.

121. If a broker establishes an account to hold money belonging to others, which of the following is correct?

    1. Accounts may be labeled either "trust" or "savings."
    2. All checks, deposit slips, and bank statements must include the word "escrow" or "trust" as part of the account name.
    3. The account cannot be in the same bank as the broker's personal checking account.
    4. An individual account is required for each transaction.

122. A broker manages three properties for the same owner. One property is in need of emergency repairs, but there is not enough money in the management account to cover the cost. The broker borrows money from the escrow account of one of the other properties to make the repairs. Which of the following is true?

    1. The broker has acted properly by safeguarding the client's interest.
    2. Such action is proper when the same person owns all properties.
    3. The broker is in violation of regulations for improperly handling escrow funds.
    4. The broker must use personal funds for repairs if there is not enough money in the management account.

123. Twenty days after a buyer and seller created a sales contract, the buyer defaulted on the contract. The contract stated that if the buyer refuses to close according to the terms of the contract, the seller may declare the buyer in default and the earnest money to be divided equally between the seller and the listing agent. The seller declared the buyer in default and the broker disbursed the $2,000 earnest money from the escrow account as follows: a check to the seller for half of the $1,000 earnest money, a check for $500 to his company operating account as commission to the company, and a check for $500 to his affiliate broker, who listed the property for sale, as commission. All of the following are true EXCEPT that the broker

    1. may disburse funds by a reasonable interpretation of the contract.
    2. acted properly in giving the seller half the earnest money in accordance with the contract.
    3. acted properly in paying to his operating account a check for his share of the earnest money.
    4. acted properly in paying his affiliate broker his or her share of the commission from the escrow account.

124. A broker opened his escrow account as an interest-bearing account with the bank. What do the Tennessee license laws say about having an interest-bearing escrow account?

1. The broker may keep any interest earned by the funds and remove them from the account at closing.
2. The broker may keep the earnest money but must let it remain in the account until the next calendar year.
3. The license laws of Tennessee neither require nor prohibit an interest-bearing escrow account.
4. The broker should split the interest with the buyer and seller.

125. The owner of XYZ Realty is not a real estate licensee. The owner hires a licensed broker as the employing broker and shares signing rights to the escrow account. The owner periodically writes checks against the escrow account for his personal use and within a week replaces the funds. No buyer or seller has been injured as a result of his activities. Which of the following is correct?

1. The owner of the firm has a right to be on the account and may use the funds so long as the funds are replaced promptly.
2. The broker may have his license revoked by the commission.
3. The broker may never allow the non-licensee owner to have check-writing authority on the escrow account.
4. The owner may not even make deposits to the account.

126. State law requires that a preprinted offer to purchase that is intended to become a binding contract have which of the following headings?

1. No particular heading is required by law in Tennessee
2. Offer to Purchase
3. Standard Purchase Offer and Contract
4. Purchase Offer Form

127. In Tennessee, brokers and salespeople who are not lawyers may

1. complete a bill of sale and deed after a sales contract has been signed.
2. fill in blanks on preprinted form contracts customarily used in their community.
3. review a buyer's present rental lease and tell them how to get out of it in order to buy a residence.
4. explain the legal significance of specific preprinted contract clauses to a buyer or seller.

128. Which of the following forms, when required by law, must be completely filled out by the seller and signed by the seller and made available to all prospective buyers?

1. Subagency agreement
2. The Tennessee Residential Property Condition Disclosure
3. Radon disclosure form
4. Statement that the property has not been the site of a homicide, suicide, or felony

129. A broker signs a listing agreement with a seller. The agreement contains the following clause: "If the property has not been sold after three months from the date of this signing, this agreement will automatically continue for additional three-month periods thereafter or until the property is sold." Based on these facts, the agreement

    1. is legal under Tennessee law, because it contains a reference to a specific time limit.
    2. is illegal in Tennessee.
    3. automatically receives a statutory six-month listing period in Tennessee.
    4. is legal under Tennessee law, because the list periods are for less than six months each.

130. Regarding listing agreements in Tennessee, which of the following could result in the suspension or revocation of a licensee's license to practice real estate?

    1. Specified commission rate
    2. No specific termination date
    3. No broker protection clause
    4. Specific termination date

131. Under Tennessee law, which of the following disclosures must be given to the seller prior to the signing of a listing if an agency agreement is not a part of the listing?

    1. Number of years the company has been in business
    2. Fact that the licensee is a REALTOR®
    3. Disposition of earnest money in the event of a purchaser default
    4. Licensee's buyer's agency or facilitator status

132. Upon obtaining a listing, a broker or licensed affiliate broker is obligated to

    1. set up a listing file and issue it a sequential number in compliance with Tennessee real estate license law and rules.
    2. place advertisements in the local newspapers.
    3. cooperate with every real estate office wishing to participate in the marketing of the listed property.
    4. give the sellers signing the listing a legible, signed, true, and correct copy immediately upon the execution of their signatures.

133. A seller listed his house for sale with a broker on February 1. The listing agreement was to last five months. In April, the seller decided that the house was no longer for sale and notified the broker he was canceling the listing agreement. The seller

    1. has canceled the agreement and there is no recourse for the broker.
    2. has withdrawn the broker's authority to sell the property and may be liable for compensation to the broker.
    3. is required by law to leave his house on the market until June.
    4. may submit the matter to the Tennessee Real Estate Commission to determine the legality of the cancellation.

134. An affiliate broker engaged in activities that constitute violations of the Tennessee Human Rights Act, including blockbusting and discrimination on the basis of a handicap. She also cashed a $25,000 earnest money check from a prospective buyer and used the proceeds to buy a new car. The affiliate broker's employing broker was unaware of all of these activities. What is the impact on the employing broker when the affiliate broker's violations are brought to the attention of the Tennessee Real Estate Commission?

    1. The employing broker may not have his or her license revoked as a result of the affiliate broker's violations.
    2. The employing broker will be required to pay any fine imposed against the affiliate broker out of his or her own personal funds.
    3. The affiliate broker's actions are legally the responsibility of the employing broker, who will be subject to the same disciplinary action as the affiliate broker whether or not he or she knew the violations had occurred.
    4. The affiliate broker's employing broker will be held liable for the Tennessee Human Rights Act violations only.

135. A person who believes that he or she has been illegally discriminated against may file a complaint with the Tennessee

    1. Board of REALTORS®.
    2. Attorney General.
    3. Real Estate Commission.
    4. Human Rights Commission or HUD.

136. A housing discrimination charge must be filed with the Tennessee Human Rights Commission within what time frame from the alleged discriminatory practice?

    1. 30 days
    2. 3 months
    3. 180 days
    4. 2 years

137. If a seller tells his listing agent he is selling his property because he believes he has AIDS, which of the following statements is true in Tennessee?

    1. The broker should include this fact in the sales contract.
    2. The broker should not include this fact in the sales contract.
    3. In Tennessee, brokers are permitted to add additional clauses to the sales contract to ensure everyone is aware of the possibility of this disease being transmitted to the new owner by the occupancy of such a building.
    4. Under Tennessee law, a notice that the seller had AIDS would void the contract.

138. A Tennessee real estate affiliate broker may lawfully collect compensation for real estate services requiring a license from

    1. either a buyer or a seller.
    2. his or her employing broker only.
    3. any party to the transaction or the party's representative.
    4. a licensed real estate broker only.

139. What are the procedures that an affiliate broker must follow when the affiliate decides to terminate his or her affiliation with the employing broker?

    1. Give the broker an official letter of termination that he or she can send to the real estate commission
    2. Complete TREC Form 1 by filling out the required blocks, obtain the releasing and accepting brokers' signatures, post his or her license on the new broker's office wall, and transmit the form and proper fee to the real estate commission
    3. Return all customer cards to the employing broker
    4. Return his or her license, along with a letter of termination, to the real estate commission

140. A licensed affiliate broker may hold a concurrent license with more than one Tennessee broker under which of the following circumstances?

    1. Under no circumstances
    2. With the permission of his or her sales manager
    3. With the written consent of the brokers being represented
    4. With the permission of the real estate commission

141. Several weeks after a closing, an affiliate broker received a "thank you" letter and a nice bonus check from the seller of the house. The affiliate broker cashed the check because he felt it was well earned. In this situation, which of the following is true?

    1. The affiliate broker may accept the bonus because he is licensed as an affiliate broker.
    2. Accepting the money is allowed if more than 30 days have elapsed since the closing.
    3. The affiliate broker may accept the money if his broker permits him to do so.
    4. Accepting the money is a violation of commission regulations.

142. When a sole proprietor broker has his or her license suspended for two years, what effect does this have on the affiliate brokers and other brokers affiliated with the proprietor?

    1. Affiliates' licenses will be revoked, subject to reinstatement after one year.
    2. Affiliates' licenses will also be suspended for a two-year period.
    3. Suspension has no effect on the affiliates.
    4. Affiliates' licenses are subject to suspension.

143. A broker intends to open a branch office in a neighboring town. The broker applies for a branch office license, giving a name that clearly identifies its relationship with his main office. The broker names a licensed real estate affiliate broker as the branch office manager. Under these facts, will the broker receive approval for the branch office?

    1. Yes, the broker has fully complied with the requirements of the license law.
    2. Yes, by naming the affiliate broker as the branch's manager, the broker is in compliance with the requirement that a broker may be in direct operational control of only one office or branch.
    3. No, the manager of a branch office must be a licensed real estate broker.
    4. No, under the license law, brokers cannot have branch offices in more than one municipality.

144. An affiliate broker is not satisfied with her present real estate company and has decided to become associated with another company. Before the affiliate broker can begin actively selling for the new company, the

    1. first broker must transfer the associate broker's license to the new office.
    2. new broker must notify the commission of the change and send in the proper forms and fees.
    3. associate broker must take her license to the new brokerage and notify the commission, within three days, of the transfer to a new location.
    4. affiliate broker must send the commission the TREC Form 1, signed by the old and new brokers, along with the proper fee.

145. When a licensed broker changes his or her place of business,

    1. a new license will be issued by the commission immediately.
    2. his or her license may be revoked if the commission is not notified within ten days.
    3. a new license will be issued for a full term.
    4. the new address does not require documentation from the proper zoning authority.

146. In any real estate sales transaction that a broker negotiates, the broker is required to do all of the following EXCEPT

    1. make sure that the written purchase and sales agreement includes all the terms of the parties' agreement.
    2. make sure that the closing statement is accurate and that a copy of it is delivered to both buyer and seller if he or she personally conducts the closing.
    3. inform the buyer of his or her personal opinion of the condition of the seller's title to the property.
    4. keep copies of all documents involved in the transaction in his or her files for three years after the year in which the transaction was closed.

147. All of the following are necessary for a broker to be entitled to a commission EXCEPT a(n)

    1. signed listing agreement.
    2. offer to purchase the property at full price and terms from a ready, willing, and able buyer.
    3. active real estate license.
    4. contract with someone to get paid for the service.

148. How much of the broker's personal money may be kept in an escrow or trust account?

    1. None
    2. Only an amount sufficient to keep the account open when all other funds have been disbursed
    3. Not more than $50
    4. Not more than $25

149. Every Tennessee real estate office is required to

    1. maintain escrow account records for five years.
    2. keep transaction records for three years.
    3. display signage inside the office.
    4. employ at least one affiliate broker.

150. Under the terms of a sales contract, a seller is required to provide a termite certificate. The seller requests that the affiliate broker order one. The affiliate broker does so, knowing she will receive a referral fee from the pest control company. Is this a violation of the license law?

    1. No, if the fee is less than $25
    2. No, if the fee is disclosed, either orally or in writing, to the parties to the contract
    3. Yes, because the affiliate broker may not receive a fee from anyone other than her employing broker
    4. Yes, because only the seller may pay special fees to the affiliate broker

151. An airline pilot, who does not hold a real estate license, told a broker about some friends who were looking for a new home. The broker contacted the friends and eventually sold them a house. When may the broker pay the airline pilot for this valuable lead?

    1. As soon as a valid sales contract is signed by the parties
    2. Only after the sale closes
    3. After the funds are released from escrow
    4. At no time may the broker pay the airline pilot for the lead

152. A broker is convicted on May 1 of possession and distribution of a controlled substance. Both the crime and the conviction took place out of state. On July 15, the broker calls the real estate commission and leaves a message informing the real estate commission of the conviction. Based on these facts, which of the following is true?

    1. The broker has properly informed the real estate commission of the conviction, and the broker's license may be renewed.
    2. The broker's failure to notify the commission of the conviction within 60 days violates real estate commission regulations and the license is automatically terminated.
    3. Because the conviction did not occur in Tennessee, it is not evidence of unworthy conduct.
    4. The conviction is evidence of both improper dealing and fraud.

153. Is an applicant who passes an examination necessarily qualified for licensure?

    1. Yes
    2. Yes, so long as he submits it within six months of passing the test
    3. Yes, if the applicant has a sponsoring broker
    4. No

154. A buyer has just entered into a contract to buy a condominium unit from a person who originally bought the unit from the developer and has lived there for the past ten years. This new buyer has a right to cancel the contract within

    1. 5 days of receipt of resale documents.
    2. 15 days of receipt of resale documents.
    3. 5 days from the date of the newly executed contract.
    4. The new buyer does not have the right to cancel a signed contract in this situation without a legal excuse and may be compelled by a court to comply with the terms of the contract.

155. In Tennessee, the amount of real estate commissions charged to clients is

    1. set by law.
    2. set by the Tennessee Real Estate Commission.
    3. determined by local groups of brokers.
    4. negotiable between the seller and the broker or the buyer and the broker.

156. A broker received an earnest money deposit from a buyer on an accepted offer. Under Tennessee law, the broker should

    1. open a special, separate escrow account that will contain funds for this transaction only, separate from funds received in any other transaction.
    2. deposit the money in an existing special escrow account in which all earnest money received from buyers may be held at the same time.
    3. immediately (or by the next business day) commingle the funds by depositing the earnest money in the broker's personal interest-bearing checking or savings account.
    4. hold the earnest money deposit in the listing folder in the broker's real estate office until the offer is accepted.

157. As of July 1, 2005, newly licensed brokers must complete 120 hours of post education

    1. within two years of license issuance.
    2. within three years of license issuance and then there are no further education requirements.
    3. within three years of license issuance and thereafter the same 16 hours requirement of affiliate brokers.
    4. within three years of license issuance and another 120 hours every three years thereafter.

158. A broker manages two properties for the same owner. The broker's fee as stated in the contact is eight percent of the rent. The broker now wants to renegotiate his commission to 10 percent of the rent on the second property because of added expenses. Which of the following is correct?

    1. It is too late; once the contract is signed, the broker must continue managing the properties at the eight percent rate.
    2. Such action cannot be changed.
    3. If they both agree, the broker and the owner may mutually renegotiate the management contract.
    4. The broker must release the owner from the management agreement.

159. A seller complained to the commission that he now believes the listing broker broke the law in charging a 15 percent commission for the sale of his vacant ten-acre parcel of property. The commission ordered the broker to reduce the commission to 10 percent. Which of the following is correct?

    1. The broker must follow the commission's order.
    2. The broker acted improperly in charging more than the standard 6 percent commission.
    3. The broker's actions were proper in charging the standard 15 percent commission for lots and acreage.
    4. All of the commissioners shall forfeit their licenses.

160. How many trust or escrow accounts must a broker maintain?

    1. One
    2. Two; one for residential and one for commercial property security deposits
    3. Three; one for residential, one for commercial, and one for apartments
    4. None; if the broker does not routinely hold earnest money, such as a buyer agency only

161. All of the following must appear in a written listing agreement EXCEPT

    1. a statement that the property must be shown to all prospective buyers regardless of race, color, religion, national origin, sex, handicap, or familial status.
    2. the complete legal description of the property being sold.
    3. the time duration of the listing.
    4. the proposed gross sale price of the property.

162. What is the redemption time after a property has been sold at a trust deed foreclosure?

    1. Six months
    2. One year
    3. Three years
    4. None

163. Regarding listing agreements in Tennessee, which of the following could result in the suspension or revocation of a licensee's license to practice real estate?

    1. Specified commission rate
    2. Working for a broker who is under a retired license
    3. No broker protection clause
    4. Specified termination date

164. Under Tennessee law, may a company take a listing as a transactional broker instead of serving as the seller's agent?

   1. Yes, but they must default to dual agency when showing the property to a buyer.
   2. Yes, the company may serve as a transactional broker throughout the listing period.
   3. No, the company must serve as the seller's agent throughout the listing period.
   4. No, the REALTOR® firm must assign an affiliate to act as a designated agent.

165. Upon obtaining a listing, a broker or licensed salesperson is obligated to

   1. send out notices to other brokers in the area.
   2. place advertisements in statewide newspapers.
   3. buy the property if no one else does.
   4. use his or her best efforts to sell the property.

166. Errors and omissions insurance

   1. must be purchased by all licensees on an annual basis.
   2. must be purchased immediately upon license issuance.
   3. expires December 31 of each even-numbered year and must be renewed by November 1 of that year for the following two years.
   4. expires on the same date of expiration of the license.

167. A sales contract is signed and copies are given to all parties on May 1. No date for payment of the commission was stated in the sales agreement. Closing takes place on June 10, and the deed of trust is recorded on June 15 by a closing attorney. When was the commission earned by the broker?

   1. June 10
   2. May 1
   3. June 15
   4. August 30

168. In Tennessee, who is responsible, prior to closing, for calculating the prorations between the buyer and seller, searching the title, and preparing the deed?

   1. Seller
   2. Affiliate broker
   3. Closing attorney
   4. Lender

169. A broker or affiliate broker may perform all of the following in preparation for the closing EXCEPT

   1. maintain a time schedule and provide net data.
   2. explain closing procedures to both buyer and seller and anticipate decision-making alternatives.
   3. coordinate inspections and deliver documents and escrow monies to the appropriate attorney.
   4. conduct any title searches that might be required and render an opinion of title.

170. A broker decides he wants to conduct the closing on an all-cash sale of a property between his client, the seller, and the buyer, his customer. With these parties, the broker

    1. must use either an attorney or a title company.
    2. must use an attorney-at-law.
    3. must use an attorney-in-fact since the buyer is a customer.
    4. may conduct the closing.

171. An aggrieved person is awarded a judgment against a real estate licensee for violation of the Tennessee Real Estate Broker Act of 1973. Regarding the real estate education and recovery account, the aggrieved party has the right to

    1. immediately apply to the real estate commission for payment from the real estate education and recovery account for the full judgment amount plus court costs and attorney's fees.
    2. a maximum award amount of $50,000 from the real estate education and recovery account, including court costs and attorney's fees.
    3. seek satisfaction from the licensee in a private civil action after being compensated from the real estate education and recovery account.
    4. receive up to a $15,000 maximum recovery from the real estate education and recovery account, if so directed by a court order.

172. The purpose of the Tennessee Real Estate Education and Recovery Account is to

    1. ensure that Tennessee real estate licensees have adequate funds available to pay their licensing and continuing education fees.
    2. provide a means of compensation for actual monetary losses suffered by individuals as a result of the acts of a licensee in violating the license law or committing other illegal acts related to a real estate transaction.
    3. protect the Tennessee Real Estate Commission from claims by individuals that they have suffered a monetary loss as the result of the action of a licensee in violating the license law or committing other illegal acts related to a real estate transaction.
    4. provide an interest-generating source of revenue to fund the activities of the real estate commission.

173. The maximum liability of the Tennessee Real Estate Education and Recovery Account for any single transaction, regardless of the number of persons aggrieved or parcels of real estate involved in such transaction, shall not exceed

    1. $5,000.
    2. $10,000.
    3. $15,000.
    4. $50,000.

174. A real estate licensee (broker, affiliate broker, or time share salesperson) is found financially liable in four lawsuits involving several different transactions. The court orders payment from the Real Estate Education and Recovery Account for the judgments. What is the maximum that can be paid to the consumers on behalf of the broker, affiliate broker, or time share salesperson for these judgments?

   1. $5,000
   2. $10,000
   3. $30,000
   4. $50,000

175. Whenever the commission is required to satisfy a claim against a licensee with money from the real estate education and recovery account, they may revoke the licensee's license. In the event that this happens, the

   1. licensee may continue engaging in real estate activities under the commission's direct supervision.
   2. licensee must repay the full amount plus interest to the account if his or her license is to be reinstated.
   3. aggrieved party may later collect additional damages by forcing the sale of any property newly acquired by the defendant licensee.
   4. licensee must thereafter pay $25 per year into the account when applying to renew his or her license.

176. What is the minimum balance of the Tennessee Real Estate Education and Recovery Account?

   1. $400,000
   2. $500,000
   3. $600,000
   4. $750,000

177. After proper investigation or upon a court order to the commission, a payment is made from the real estate education and recovery account due to the improper activities of a licensee. What happens when the payment is made?

   1. The licensee's license may be suspended or revoked, at the discretion of the commission.
   2. The commission takes no further action if the licensee repays the fund within 30 days.
   3. The licensee's license is automatically revoked.
   4. The licensee is subject to a fine of $2,000.

178. A broker of a firm has errors and omissions insurance for herself. Is E&O insurance also required on the firm?

   1. Yes, the commission requires that all affiliate brokers, brokers, and firms have E&O insurance.
   2. No, only affiliate brokers are required to have E&O insurance.
   3. Yes, there are never any exceptions.
   4. No, the firm is not required to have insurance, only the licensees.

179. An affiliate renewed his license and E&O insurance two months late and paid the required penalty fees. He is now being sued for an event that happened during the last licensing period. He was insured when the event occurred and is insured as the lawsuit is being filed against him. Is the affiliate covered by insurance for this event?

   1. No, his insurance will not cover the claim against him.
   2. Yes, he is covered. He was insured at both times.
   3. Yes, he paid his penalty fees and reinstated his license.
   4. No, the insurance company will not accept him.

180. A licensed broker has decided to put her license in temporary retirement. Is the broker required to continue to carry E&O insurance?

     1. Yes, she must carry the insurance, but she has the option of obtaining it independently.
     2. Yes, she must carry the insurance, but she must purchase it from the E&O insurance company that has the state contract.
     3. No, it is not available to licensees who have their licenses in temporary retirement.
     4. No, licensees who have their licenses in temporary retirement are not required to carry E&O insurance.

181. The commission was unable to obtain E&O insurance for all licensees who chose to participate in the insurance program. In this situation,

     1. the requirement for these licensees to have insurance is void until such time that it is available.
     2. franchise real estate companies must have insurance provided to them by their parent franchiser.
     3. independent real estate companies must obtain insurance from local insurance companies.
     4. all real estate licensees must obtain E&O insurance independently if the commission is unable to obtain it for them.

182. Broker Z's client, the purchaser, is suing Broker Z for misstating the square footage of the home that was purchased. Broker Z's errors and omissions insurance company wants to settle the claim without going to court and Broker Z refuses the company's request, insisting the claim is excessive. Which of the following is true?

     1. The insurance company must represent him and cover any judgment awarded to the client up to the maximum amount of the insurance policy.
     2. The insurance company can refuse to represent him if he does not agree to settle the claim out of court.
     3. Broker Z should cancel his insurance and sue the insurance company.
     4. The company will represent Broker Z, but is only required to pay a claim up to the amount that they were willing to settle for out of court. Any amount over that will be at Broker Z's expense.

183. When listing a property, a listing agent observed water pooling under the conventional foundation of the building during a rainstorm. Three days later, the water dried up and did not return. There has been no rainfall since that date. In the showing and sale of the property, all of the following statements are true EXCEPT that

    1. the listing agent has a duty to inquire about the water settlement with his seller.
    2. the listing agent has no duty to inform a buyer, buyer's agent, or facilitator showing the property about the water settlement under the building if it has dried up and does not appear to have caused any damage.
    3. the listing agent must advise any potential buyer, buyer's agent, or facilitator showing the property about the settlement of water during rainstorms.
    4. the listing agent should consider this to be a latent defect.

184. A buyer wants to see a house listed by XYZ Realty. Affiliate Broker K of XYZ Realty greets the buyer and offers to show the property to him. K did not personally list the property for sale for his broker. In this situation, affiliate Broker K

    1. may sign up the buyer with a buyer agency agreement and then represent the buyer and show him the property specified earlier by the buyer.
    2. may sign up the buyer with a dual agency agreement and then show him the property.
    3. must sign up the buyer with a designated agency agreement prior to showing him the property.
    4. may show the property to the buyer and treat him as a customer.

185. K, an affiliate broker of XYZ Realty, meets a customer who inquires about K's listing. The buyer told K that he was willing to pay full price for the property and then asked if K would represent him. K then advised him that she was the seller's agent and would show him the property, but would only treat him as a customer. After looking at the property, the buyer requested that she write up the offer for less than the listed price. Which of the following is correct?

    1. When presenting the offer, K must tell her seller that the buyer could pay full price for the property.
    2. K may not write up the offer for less than the list price if she is the seller's agent.
    3. K may refuse to present any offer that did not meet her seller's requirements.
    4. K may not tell her seller that the buyer was willing to pay full price.

186. The prospective buyer asked affiliate broker K if she would be his agent to assist and advise him in the purchase of a residence. What action should K take to establish a buyer agency with this prospective buyer?

    1. K may tell the buyer that her company will serve as his agent and proceed to show him suitable properties.
    2. K must tell the buyer that as of that moment, her company is his agent and will tell all other companies of her buyer agency status.
    3. K must first have the buyer sign a Confirmation of Agency Status Form to establish the agency.
    4. K must first execute a bilateral agency agreement with the buyer to establish the buyer agency relationship.

187. New affiliate broker J just received his Tennessee license and posted it on the broker's office wall. The broker explained the commission split that J would make and told him he was now an agent of the company. No written agreements were signed between the broker and affiliate broker J. During the next two weeks J gave six listing presentations to sellers and obtained four listings for the company. As a result of J's outstanding performance how many new listings does the company now have?

   1. Zero
   2. None; they are all J's
   3. Two for J and two for the company
   4. Four

188. Regarding the agency status of a "facilitator," a facilitator represents

   1. the buyer.
   2. the seller.
   3. both the buyer and the seller.
   4. neither the buyer nor the seller. There has been no creation of agency status.

189. A broker's real estate company only represents buyers and does not list property for sale. The broker requires that all agents within the company only work with buyers who will sign a buyer agency agreement. They further agree in the contract to never default to another status or request a change in their relationship with the buyer. What form of agency does this establish?

   1. Facilitator
   2. Single agency as a buyer's agent
   3. Designated agency
   4. Dual agency

190. A real estate broker verbally tells the buyer that the broker will be his agent. The broker then shows the buyer a property listed with another firm and writes an offer that is accepted. Later, the buyer pays a commission to the broker. Who did the broker represent?

   1. Buyer
   2. Seller
   3. Both the buyer and the seller
   4. No one

191. The broker in XYZ Realty has obtained an agency listing for the company to sell a dental office. A customer called about the property and wants to look at it. The broker tells the customer that since he has no written agency agreement with the customer, he will show it as a facilitator. Prior to preparing the offer, the broker has the customer acknowledge his facilitator status in writing and gives the customer a copy of the written disclosure statement. In this scenario, the broker

   1. is performing in a professional manner.
   2. can act as a facilitator to the buyer, and agent to the seller.
   3. misrepresented himself.
   4. represents the customer.

192. After a sales call, a buyer came to the office. The broker gave the prospect the state-required pamphlet explaining the duties owed to a customer and a client. The broker never offered to serve as the buyer's agent. The broker sold the buyer, P, a property that was listed through the broker's firm. Prior to showing the property, the broker disclosed his seller's agency status and the buyer signed the disclosure form prior to the preparation of the offer. A month after the buyer purchased the property, he complained to the commission that the broker should have offered to represent him. What penalty may the commission levy against the broker for his actions?

   1. The broker may be downgraded to affiliate broker status for failure to represent the buyer.
   2. Because this is his first offense, the broker may receive a letter of reprimand for his improper conduct.
   3. The broker may be assigned additional continuing education courses as punishment.
   4. The broker did nothing wrong and the complaint is frivolous.

193. Within the same real estate firm, two different affiliate brokers obtained agency contracts for their company. One agency agreement was with a landlord to lease office space. The other agency agreement was with a tenant to find office space. All of the following are ways to show the landlord client's office space to the tenant client EXCEPT

   1. obtain written permission from both clients to act as a dual agent.
   2. obtain written permission from both clients to serve as a facilitator.
   3. obtain written permission from both clients to serve as designated agents.
   4. obtain written permission from both clients to serve as both a landlord agent and a tenant agent.

194. Tennessee law recognizes all of the following forms of ownership EXCEPT

   1. community property rights.
   2. tenancy by the entireties.
   3. tenancy in severalty.
   4. tenancy in common.

195. Which of the following life estates are recognized in Tennessee?

   1. Curtesy
   2. Dower
   3. Community property
   4. Conventional life estates

196. Who determines the rate of the transfer tax?

   1. County commissioners
   2. Legislature
   3. Agreement between buyer and seller
   4. Governor

197. Property tax due dates

    1. are determined annually by the legislature.
    2. vary in every city and county in the state.
    3. are December 31, paid in advance.
    4. are December 31, paid in arrears.

198. A seller was unaware that his agent misrepresented the seller's property to the buyer. The buyer suffered damages as a result of this misrepresentation. Which of the following is correct?

    1. The seller is liable for the representations of his agent.
    2. Only if the agent is working as a dual agent will the seller be liable for the agent's actions.
    3. Only if the seller's agent is working as a designated agent will the seller be liable for the agent's actions.
    4. The seller is not liable for the misrepresentations of his agent unless the seller knew or had reasons to know of the misrepresentations.

Answer Key

1. 2. The Tennessee Real Estate Commission administers the real estate license law. The Tennessee Human Rights Commission handles fair housing complaints; the Tennessee Association of REALTORS® is a trade association; and HUD is a federal government agency that supervises housing issues.

2. 1. The governor makes the appointments. The Tennessee Association of REALTORS® is a trade association and neither it nor the public elects the commission members.

3. 2. The legislature enacts law; the Tennessee Real Estate Commission is authorized to write rules and regulations that have the force of law. An independent testing service writes the exam questions and administers the exams.

4. 2. The commission may not initiate a random search for investigations of licensees. There must be some valid reason. If a member of the public files a complaint, the commission will review the complaint, and if merited, the commission will forward the complaint to the respondent for a reply within ten days.

5. 2. The members of the commission are appointed by the governor for a term of five years.

6. 3. The state association of REALTORS® is not a governmental body and therefore has no power to appoint the commission members or control the licenses of state licensed brokers and affiliate brokers. The commission makes and enforces rules. The exams are written under the supervision of the commission and administered by an independent testing company. An executive director administers the operations of the commission.

7. 4. The governor appoints nine members to serve on the commission.

8. 3. The governor appoints seven members who are brokers and/or affiliate brokers.

9. 1. Two non-licensee members are selected to serve on the commission who must be from different grand divisions.

10. 4. The Tennessee Real Estate Commission meets regularly each month for up to three days per session depending upon the amount of required business.

11. 3. The commission has a full-time legal counsel and a full-time director of education. The governor appoints the commission; he or she does not serve them. The commission may refer a complaint to a court of competent jurisdiction; however, the courts do not serve the commission. The Appraisal Commission is separate from the Tennessee Real Estate Commission.

12. 3. The Tennessee Real Estate Commission is a part of the Department of Commerce and Insurance, located at 500 James Robertson Road, Nashville, Tennessee.

13. 1. Anyone who manages office space for lease is required to have a real estate license. Partners selling their own property and licensed attorneys holding a power of attorney do not have to have a real estate license. A resident manager or an employee of the owner or broker is specifically exempted from licensing requirements provided it is just one employer and just one apartment, duplex, or residential complex and they do not negotiate the terms of a lease or the amount of the security deposit.

14. 2. Receipt of anything of value, even a sewing machine, for selling other people's real estate requires a real estate license. The resident manager is specifically exempt from being required to have a real estate license for the above-specified act, and court-appointed trustees are not required to have a real estate license.

15. 2. Any person who holds a securities dealer's license must obtain a real estate license just like anyone else who brokers real estate. Similarly, when a real estate broker is offering real estate to a certain number of investors, a security dealer's license is also required.

16. 2. Members of a partnership, association, or corporation must have a real estate license if they are conducting real estate brokerage business; one of them must be a broker. Filing papers with the secretary of state is a requirement for incorporation, not for real estate licensing.

17. 2. A person who is reselling a mobile home is not required to hold a real estate license because the mobile home itself is considered to be personal property. A real estate license is required to manage commercial real estate, bring together buyers and sellers for a fee, and/or collect rents.

18. 2. Attorneys at law are exempt from real estate licensing when acting as attorneys; however, they must obtain a real estate license to broker real estate. Appraisers, associations, partnerships, corporations, and real property securities dealers, if engaging in real estate activities, must have a real estate license.

19. 4. In Tennessee, the term "manager" is reserved for the managing broker who must be licensed as a broker and registered with the commission as such. The activities specified in the question are clerical in nature and may be delegated by the broker to a non-licensed person.

20. 1. In Tennessee, applications for any real estate license must be completed within six months after taking the written exam, or the exam must be retaken and passed before being licensed. Testing is done on an ongoing basis throughout the year. Sworn statements and letters of recommendation are not required to take the test.

21. 3. Being actively engaged as a licensed affiliate broker for at least four years is not a requirement for obtaining a broker's license in Tennessee. Completing 120 hours of approved courses, being at least 18 years old, and being of good moral character are all required for licensure.

22. 2. An applicant has six months from the date of passing the exam to apply for his or her license; in this example, the applicant has until July 15, 2005.

23. 4. The licensee cannot sue the seller, because N did not have an active broker license at the time the agreement was reached. N was not even an affiliate broker.

24. 2. One does not need a real estate license to sell personal property, i.e., stock equipment, but does need one to sell the property that is permanently attached to the ground, such as a building. Owners are not required to obtain real estate licenses to manage their own properties. The superintendent of a large apartment building is specifically exempt from being required to have a real estate license. A person who has a recorded power of attorney need not obtain a real estate license in order to negotiate the sale of the parent's residence.

25. 3. Persons with a past criminal record must request a hearing before the commission prior to being licensed. The commission may permit the applicant to be licensed, depending upon the outcome of the hearing.

26. 2. An individual who receives compensation for procuring prospective buyers or renters of real estate must hold a real estate license.

27. 1. Property owners who rent, sell, or buy property for themselves are exempt from licensing requirements.

28. 4. As of January 1, 2005, a candidate applying for a Tennessee real estate license must successfully complete a 60-hour course in the general principles of real estate, pass the state exam, complete the 30-hour New Affiliate Broker Course and purchase errors and omissions insurance. The courses may be online computer courses, classroom courses, or correspondence courses accredited by the Commission. The candidate must then be sponsored by a licensed broker.

29. 3. The Tennessee Real Estate Commission, through the Department of Commerce and Insurance, issues all real estate licenses.

30. 4. All new licenses issued after July 1, 2005, expire every other year or the anniversary date of the individual affiliate broker's license. Those licenses issued prior to that date will be staggered to ultimately expire on a two-year anniversary date.

31. 2. To qualify to take the real estate broker's examination, a candidate must be at least 18 years of age, have held an active affiliate broker's license for at least 36 months, complete 120 hours of approved education (30 hours of which must be the broker office management course), and receive permission from the commission to take the exam. If the candidate has a 4-year college degree, with a major in real estate, the candidate only needs 24 months of an active license instead of 36 months.

32. 3. The maximum penalty is $1,000 per day for each separate violation in addition to other penalties provided by law.

33. 1. The Core Course of 4 hours and 12 additional hours of commission-approved courses must be completed prior to each renewal period by affiliate brokers.

34. 4. After the first renewal of a license in Tennessee, affiliate brokers must take the current 4-hour Core Course and 12 additional hours of continuing education during that period and every two years thereafter to renew their license for the following two years.

35. 1. When the license expires, there is no "free" time in which to renew without penalties.

36. 4. Errors and omissions insurance expires on the last day of each even-numbered year. Proof of E&O insurance for the next two years must be sent to the Commission and postmarked no later than November 1 of each even-numbered year.

37. 4. None; as of January 1, 2005, the mandatory "New Affiliate Broker Course" must be completed prior to license issuance.

38. 4. The commission, in its discretion, may refuse to issue, renew, or reinstate a license. The commission cannot require a licensee to move to or from Tennessee.

39. 2. You are required to disclose your name, company name, and your representational status. You should not disclose confidential information about your client such as the maximum amount they are willing to pay. The rate of commission payable to the selling agent is usually offered by the listing company, but it is still negotiable.

40. 3. Generally, reciting published information, such as price and location of a specific property, is considered ministerial and may be performed by a non-licensed person. However, non-licensed persons may only give out information on the listing as limited by the broker.

41. 3. Informational services may be performed by a non-licensee. Only a licensee may perform services that are transactional, routine brokerage, and even customer-level service.

42. 3. Only a licensed person may explain simple contract documents to prospective buyers. Administrative work, bookkeeping, and writing advertising under the direction of a licensee and their broker do not require a license.

43. 2. Secretarial work such as inserting factual information into form contracts under the employing broker's supervision and approval does not require licensing since it is done under the supervision of the broker. Personal assistants may be licensed in order to perform more services for the licensee who hired them, but they do not have to be licensed to work as assistants. Only licensed personal assistants may independently host open houses.

44. 3. The broker may not compensate the assistant for participating in an activity requiring a license, such as allowing the assistant to negotiate a real estate contract or to encourage others to accept an offer. The broker may not compensate an unlicensed person based on the broker's real estate activity. Both the broker and assistant are in violation of the commission's policy regarding unlicensed assistants.

45. 4. Both the affiliate broker and the licensee holding the open house must be licensed under the same broker. This affiliate broker may not compensate his wife or his unlicensed assistant for performing duties that require a real estate license. The showing of an offered for sale property requires a real estate license in Tennessee.

46. 3. An unlicensed real estate assistant, acting on behalf of the broker, may unlock a property for a customer. However, they may not show the property by going into the property, nor may they host open houses, host booths at fairs, or negotiate the terms of a lease.

47. 4. The unlicensed assistant may not act as a go-between with a buyer and seller for the affiliate broker. An unlicensed assistant may gather tax assessor's information and prepare a market analysis for the affiliate broker.

48. 3. An unlicensed assistant may not make cold calls for a real estate licensee.

49. 1. An unlicensed assistant may not be paid on the basis of the employing licensee's real estate activity. To receive a fee based on real estate activity, one must have a real estate license.

50. 3. The licensee and the managing broker, prior to its submission for publication, must approve all advertising prepared by an unlicensed assistant.

51. 4. Both M and J were in violation of the Tennessee license laws in that J may only be compensated through her broker, and M may not directly compensate another agent for performing real estate services. All compensation must be through the managing broker.

52. 4. Licensed real estate assistants may be paid on a commission basis or other basis for work performed for licensees within the same firm if it is paid through their managing broker. The employing licensee may not pay another affiliate directly for work done that requires a license. Licensees may be paid directly by another affiliate broker if that work does not require a license. There is no Rule 74 that applies to paying taxes. A licensee may not be compensated for work requiring a license by a broker of another firm or from anyone other than the broker with whom he or she is licensed.

53. 3. The broker must file an irrevocable consent agreement with the commission. The broker must operate an office in at least one state. Tennessee does not have reciprocity with all states. An out-of-state broker who has a regular place of business in his or her state does not have to have a place of business in Tennessee.

54. 2. A nonresident license applicant must file an irrevocable consent to suit so that action can be filed against him or her regardless of the state he or she resides in.

55. 2. All monies received belonging to others must be deposited in a trust or escrow account promptly upon acceptance of the offer, unless otherwise directed in the contract.

56. 3. The broker must immediately provide the buyers with a copy of the agreement and a receipt for their deposit. Other people's money must not be placed in a personal bank account. Completing a false, second purchase agreement for the purposes of obtaining a larger loan is prohibited under any circumstances. All written offers must be presented to the seller promptly.

57. 3. In this position, the on-site manager must be licensed in order to negotiate leases. A non-licensed manager may not negotiate the terms of a lease or the amount of the security deposit. If the on-site manager is an affiliate broker, he/she must have their broker's permission to manage the property, as the broker remains responsible for the activities of his licensees.

58. 1. The law does not require any particular heading on contracts in Tennessee.

59. 1. The ad says "if it doesn't sell in 90 days" so the broker is not obligated to buy it until the 90-day expiration. The broker must indicate all terms and special considerations so that the seller is fully informed and not surprised. The broker must also be able to substantiate his offer to purchase.

60. 3. Exclusive-right-to-sell agency agreements must be in writing. Under Tennessee law, no real estate agency or subagency can be created without a bilateral written agreement. Regarding the other answer choices, there is no such listing as a closed listing; a contract to facilitate a listing does not establish agency and if it is for less than a year, it need not be in writing; and net listings are illegal in Tennessee.

61. 1. The legal age of competence is 18 in the state of Tennessee.

62. 3. Listing Broker J is responsible. Brokers are responsible for the earnest money regardless of whether such funds are held by some other person or firm. Broker M did not turn it over to Broker J. Broker J was the only person authorized to market the property for the seller. There was no error or omission since broker M stole the money. The education and recovery account will not disburse funds without a court order.

63. 4. The broker should disburse the funds in a proper manner without unreasonable delay. The broker may not pay them to his or her operating account and then disburse them to the closing party, nor should the broker pay them to the lender or buyer just before or at closing.

64. 3. The broker must specify in the contract the name and address of the person who will actually hold the funds and the terms and conditions for disbursement of the funds. Any agreements as to what constitutes a default between the buyer and seller are by agreement of the buyer and seller and must be outlined in the agreement.

65. 4. The closing broker must provide a copy of the closing documents to each customer or client. If a title company or attorney conducts the closing, the broker is not responsible for this act. A buyer would not be entitled to a copy of the broker/seller listing agreement. A seller would not be entitled to a copy of the property survey or abstract of title.

66. 3. In Tennessee, a licensee may retake and pass the appropriate license exam (affiliate broker or broker) in lieu of completing the required continuing education requirements for the renewal of their license, provided their prior education still qualifies them to do so.

67. 3. The out-of-state broker does not have to employ a Tennessee licensee. To obtain a reciprocal license, the out-of-state broker must maintain an office in Mississippi or Tennessee, maintain an active broker's license in the state of license, and must file an irrevocable consent to suit.

68. 3. Property owners who rent, sell, or buy property for themselves are exempt from licensing requirements. Persons who hold a contractor's license do not need a license to contract to build a house for themselves or others.

69. 3. A court of competent jurisdiction is the only other body that may revoke or suspend a license. The governor appoints the commission to control the issuance of real estate licenses. The commission may issue civil penalties and may refer it to a court if it deems it appropriate. The REALTORS® association does not control the real estate licenses of its members.

70. 4. Mark's home state does not have reciprocity with Tennessee. The fact that Mark and his broker were able to obtain non-residential licenses with Mississippi will not gain them reciprocity with Tennessee because their state of residence has no agreement with Tennessee. Mark and his principal broker in his home state could not obtain Tennessee nonresident licenses. Mark cannot hold various real estate licenses under more than one broker.

71. 2. The application fee for either license is $100; the renewal fee thereafter for the license is $80.

72. 4. A license that has been revoked may be reinstated upon the consenting vote of six of the members of the commission.

73. 4. While her broker's license is still valid, she is entitled to request, in writing, to surrender her broker's license for an affiliate broker's license. If she fails to surrender her license in exchange for an affiliate broker's license while it is still valid, it will not be renewed at the next renewal period. She cannot list or sell without a valid license.

74. 1. Both P and his broker are in violation of license laws. The listing of a property for sale or lease, in anticipation of a fee, constitutes a brokerage function, which requires a license at the time of taking the listing. The real estate commission can impose a penalty of up to $1,000 per day per offense; the court can fine up to $400, award triple damages, and/or pass sentence of one year's imprisonment.

75. 2. In Tennessee, only a licensed broker may manage a real estate office. Anyone, including an affiliate broker, may own a real estate firm; however, only a broker may manage it.

76. 4. A licensee who holds a Tennessee license may sell anywhere within the state, as limited by his or her broker.

77. 1. An affiliate broker must reside within 50 miles of the firm's office, unless the broker demonstrates in writing, to the commission's satisfaction, that the distance involved is not unreasonable and that adequate supervision can be provided. Each office must have a firm license and be under the direction and supervision of a broker licensed at that address.

78. 4. She cannot work for him as an affiliate broker. Only a principal broker who is engaged primarily in the real estate business and accessible during normal working hours may engage a licensee.

79. 4. The commission will inform the licensee that the commission does not intervene in the settlement of debts, loans, draws, or commission disputes between firms, brokers, and/or affiliate brokers. The dispute could be resolved by either a prior written agreement in the original employment contract between the affiliate and the broker or a lawsuit if the parties are not REALTORS®.

80. 3. Listings are made between the broker and the seller and the affiliate is not a party to the agreement. When a licensee terminates his or her affiliation with a firm, the licensee shall neither take nor use any property listings secured through the firm unless specifically authorized by the broker. The licensee may not contact the owners of the six listings and ask them to change brokers; that would constitute interfering with the broker's business. The licensee cannot sue for the listings because they do not belong to him.

81. 1. The applicant will not be issued a license. Her application for her firm's license requires certification from the proper governmental authority and compliance with zoning laws and ordinances. Generally, zoning will not permit this business in a residential area.

82. 4. The broker is in violation of the rules of the commission. The broker must display a sign that indicates to the public that the broker is in the real estate business. The sign must be outside of the broker's place of business, even if it is also his or her home. The size of the letters on the sign is not specified in the law. The broker may have an office in his or her home if the home is in a commercially zoned area.

83. 5. The brokerage commission must be stated in the listing agreement and is negotiated between the broker and seller. Broker's commissions are not determined by law, the real estate commission, REALTORS® organizations, or by local custom.

84.   3.   A listing that does not include the price excluding the customary commission and expenses associated with the sale is illegal in Tennessee and is called a net listing. This is a good example of the conflict of interest that a net listing may provoke. Net listings are not in the best interest of the public.

85.   2.   The affiliate broker must promptly present the other agent's offer. At that time, the affiliate broker may tell the seller that he is scheduled to show it the next day. Once presented, the seller may delay any acceptance of the first offer. The affiliate broker will not be responsible if the first offeror withdraws his offer because of the delay caused by the seller. If, however, the affiliate broker failed to deliver the offer promptly, and the buyer withdrew his offer, the affiliate may be liable.

86.   1.   The affiliate broker is obligated to present all written offers to the seller until the seller has accepted one of them. The affiliate should tell the person making the verbal offer that such an offer is not enforceable and he is not required to present it. The affiliate may tell the seller about the verbal offer, but should advise him that only the written offers can become binding and enforceable. There is no working contract until an offer is accepted.

87.   4.   The broker has committed an error of omission. The seller, seeing that the buyer did not ask for the drapes in the offer, may rightfully think the buyer changed his mind and did not want them. If the broker overheard this verbal agreement, the broker should have put it in the offer.

88.   1.   The agent, by making promises, has not violated the license laws by attempting to influence the seller to do business with his firm, provided he keeps his promises. An agent may not make promises he or she cannot or does not intend to keep.

89.   4.   The buyer has a right to be informed about any material defects of the property, which are known by the seller or his agent. Disclosing known latent defects, such as a leaky roof, is not a violation of the agent's fiduciary duty of confidentiality. The rule of *caveat emptor* does not apply when selling real estate.

90.   1.   The affiliate broker has violated the license laws concerning misleading statements by claiming to be a member of organizations in which she is not, in an attempt to persuade the seller to do business with her. As a result, her license may be revoked by the commission.

91.   4.   The affiliate broker has failed to property account for funds in his possession within a reasonable time. The affiliate broker must turn the money over to his broker *immediately* upon receipt and obtain a receipt from his broker or he should have obtained a receipt for the money from the listing company upon initial presentation. The check is not being properly secured or accounted for by leaving it attached to the offer. The check cannot be placed in the office file drawer with the offer.

92.   2.   A licensee may lose his license for failing to furnish a copy of any listing, sale, lease, or other contract relevant to a real estate transaction to all signatories thereof at the time of execution. The commission would act on their complaint, sending a copy of the complaint to the broker, who must answer the complaint within ten days.

93.   4.   Tennessee law states that the licensee can lose his or her license for using a sales contract form or offer to purchase form that fails to specify a definite termination date. The earnest money must be returned to the purchaser and no commission was earned. The affiliate broker may be liable to his principal, the seller.

94. 1. The agent can lose his or her license for inducing any party to a contract to break that contract for the substitution of another contract where it is motivated by the personal gain of the licensee. The agent can be sued by the landlord and also charged with practicing law without a license.

95. 2. The agent is guilty of racial steering because he steered the couple to areas where he thought they should live and did not provide them with an alternate choice. It is not up to a licensee to decide where anyone purchasing a home should live. Regarding the other answer choices, blockbusting is an attempt to encourage owners to sell their property, inferring or charging that people of a protected class are moving in the area and it will cause a reduction in property values; and redlining is a practice of lenders wherein they do not make loans in a specified area due to the racial, ethnic, color, or religious composition of that area.

96. 4. The broker signed on the affiliate's license application that he would train and supervise her as long as her license was with him. He failed to exercise adequate supervision over the activities of his affiliate.

97. 3. There was a breach of the agent's fiduciary duty to the seller. All fees must be disclosed.

98. 4. The commission can suspend or revoke the broker's license for failing to disclose to the owner his intention or true position when offering to purchase a property listed with his office. The commission has no statutory power to rescind a sale or award damages to a member of the public.

99. 3. The broker must immediately provide the buyers with a copy of the agreement and a receipt for their deposit. Regarding the other answer choices, other people's money must not be placed in a personal bank account; completing a second earnest money/sales agreement to assist in obtaining a larger loan is illegal; and all written offers must be presented to the seller promptly.

100. 4. Commission rates are always negotiable between the seller and the broker. Commingling of funds is prohibited. The real estate commission may revoke a license if the licensee has been convicted of a felony or false advertising.

101. 4. Depositing a buyer's down payment in her own bank account would be commingling of personal and client's funds, which is a prohibited practice. An affiliate broker may represent only one broker. Buyers may be represented in today's marketplace. Most real estate brokers prefer an exclusive-listing agreement.

102. 2. Depositing earnest money into the firm's escrow account is proper procedure. Grounds for suspension or revocation include the following: mental incompetence, cheating on the licensing exam, and displaying a "For Sale" sign without the owner's consent.

103. 2. The real estate commission may suspend or revoke a licensee's license if the licensee has been found liable in a civil trial of illegal discrimination. Regarding the other answer choices, the real estate commission is only concerned about promises made that were never kept nor intended to be kept; and gifts and prizes may be offered under specific guidelines.

104. 2. A broker must always have written permission before erecting a sign on a property for sale or lease. A broker may not encourage a decision based on religious grounds and must make full disclosures of all conditions of a promotion. A licensee may lose his or her license for falsely claiming to be a member of any organization in an attempt to solicit business.

105. 4. Brokers are not to be parties to dual contracts for the purpose of fraud in obtaining a larger loan; however, if the final agreed-upon sale price is higher than originally listed, the property appraises for that higher amount, and there is no fraud present, the broker acted in a proper manner.

106. 4. All advertising is required to be in the employing broker's name (or firm's name) and must also include the broker's (firm's) telephone number. An affiliate may include his or her name as listed with the Real Estate Commission, telephone number, license number, the expiration date of his or her license, and even his or her street address, but is not required to do so. These rules apply to all advertisement media, including every page on an Internet ad.

107. 1. After obtaining written permission from the owner, the broker may erect a "For Sale" sign on the property.

108. 3. All advertising must be under the firm name and include the firm's telephone number. Ads do not have to list a box number, street address, or identify the owner of the property. Blind ads are illegal.

109. 3. When acting as a private citizen, the for-sale-by-owner licensee will not (and should not) include information about his or her employing broker. The term "owner/agent" must appear in all advertisements of property for rent or sale if owned by the licensee. Licensees may offer their own property for rent or sale without listing it with any real estate firm.

110. 1. The same rules that apply to advertising in other media also apply to the Internet. The real estate firm's name and telephone number must appear in all advertisements.

111. 1. Each page of the Web site must include the name and telephone number of the office where the affiliate broker's license is located. Tennessee license laws require the same procedure for Internet advertising as any other media.

112. 1. The brokerage commission must be stated in the listing agreement and is negotiated between the broker and seller. Brokers' commissions are not determined by law, the real estate commission, the REALTORS® organization, or by local custom.

113. 1. Brokers can and have been punished by the commission for engaging in deeds deemed improper by the commission. Brokers are responsible for the ads written by their affiliates; however, the commission does not pre-approve agents' ads.

114. 4. All licensees advertising property owned by them for sale or rent must include the designation "owner/agent." The licensee is not required to list his property through a real estate company, and he may require a security deposit from the tenant.

115. 3. Net listings are illegal at any time because of the potential conflict of interest for the broker in not serving the best interest of the public.

116. 3. A religious order may restrict the rental of the units so long as they do not discriminate in the membership of their organization.

117. 1. Commissions are always negotiable between the principal and the agent or customer and the broker, and are not determined by custom or law.

118. 4.   Other people's money, such as earnest money and security deposits, must be deposited promptly upon acceptance of the offer in accordance with the Tennessee license laws, unless the buyer and seller direct otherwise.

119. 2.   Affiliate brokers are to pay the earnest money to their broker immediately upon receipt. Monies may not be held in an unsecured place such as a listing folder, or in the company operating account.

120. 3.   Tennessee law requires that earnest money received by affiliates be delivered to the broker under whom they are employed, immediately upon receipt. The earnest money should not be shuffled back and forth with offers and counteroffers. All monies received belonging to others must be deposited in a trust or escrow account promptly upon acceptance of the offer, unless the contract calls for a later deposit date. The broker is responsible for the funds even if held by some other person or firm.

121. 2.   The account must be labeled as "escrow" or "trust" to indicate that the money in the account does not belong to the broker. A broker does not have to open a new account for each earnest money received; however, the broker must keep careful records to accurately account for all funds in the escrow or trust account.

122. 3.   The broker is in violation of regulations for improperly handling escrow funds by using funds from one property to make repairs on another property.

123. 4.   The broker may not disburse commissions to affiliates directly from the escrow account. The money should have been paid to the company operating account and then disbursed to the affiliate. The broker may disburse funds by a reasonable interpretation of the contract or pay the money to court by interpleader action. The broker may pay defaulted escrow monies to the seller from the escrow account.

124. 3.   The Tennessee license laws do not require or prohibit a broker from having an interest-bearing escrow account. The funds were not the broker's; therefore, the broker must ensure that the contract between the buyer and seller specifies which party to the contract is entitled to any interest earned by the funds. The contract should also specify who is entitled to earnest money in the event of a default of either party.

125. 2.   The broker may have his license revoked by the commission for allowing the owner to make withdrawals from the account for his own personal use, regardless of whether the funds are promptly replaced. This is called "conversion" and is a misuse of the escrow account. The owner may have check-writing authority on the account, but may not improperly use the funds. The bank will accept deposits to any account from anyone.

126. 1.   Tennessee law does not address any particular requirement.

127. 2.   The blanks in a contract form may be filled in by Tennessee licensees as directed by the customers/clients who make the final decisions and sign the contract. Licensees may also make minor additions to a contract such as counteroffers and miscellaneous items. Real estate licensees who are not lawyers must be careful to avoid any appearance of the unauthorized practice of law. The broker and salespeople are special agents, hired for a very limited purpose, which does not ordinarily include signing the name of the principal.

128. 2. The seller, when not exempt or selling a residential property "as is," must personally fill out and sign a property disclosure notice or a property disclaimer notice. The notice must be available to all prospective purchasers.

129. 2. This agreement is illegal because listings must contain a definite termination date and rollover extensions are not permitted under Tennessee law.

130. 2. All listings must have a defined termination date. Commission rates or fees are required to avoid net listings. State law does not address the issue of whether or not to include a broker protection clause.

131. 4. The licensee must disclose his or her current status to the seller as to whom, if anyone, he or she presently represents in a transaction prior to the signing of a listing agreement so as not to deceive the seller. The length of time the company has been in business and the fact that the licensee is or is not a REALTOR® is not a disclosure requirement by law. The disposition of the earnest money will be determined by agreement between the buyer and seller in the sales contract.

132. 4. The licensee is obligated to give the seller signing the listing a legible, signed, true, and correct copy of the listing agreement at the time of the signing. The numbering of the files is not required. Failure to advertise the property for sale may constitute a breach of the listing agreement and could be deemed by the commission as being an "improper act." There is no requirement to advertise it in a local newspaper. Other brokers are not required to participate in marketing.

133. 2. The listing agreement may be canceled by either party but the canceling party may be in breach of contract and therefore may be responsible for expenses or damages. The Tennessee Real Estate Commission does not have judicial decree over the seller.

134. 1. Since the broker was unaware of the affiliate broker's illegal activities, there will be no action taken against the broker by the commission. The broker is, however, responsible to train and supervise his licensees. Injured parties may have other legal remedies brought against the company.

135. 4. Fair housing complaints are generally directed to HUD or the Human Rights Commission. REALTOR® organizations and the attorney general do not receive discrimination complaints.

136. 3. A person must file a complaint with the Tennessee Human Rights Commission within 180 days of the alleged discriminatory practice.

137. 2. The disclosure of such confidential information to the seller would be a breach of fiduciary duties to a client and is prohibited by both state and federal law. Such disclosure of the seller's status may constitute an illegal discriminatory practice. Such notice alone would not void a contract (both the seller and the buyer signed the contract); however, it could leave the seller's agent open to a possible lawsuit.

138. 2. Salespeople may only collect compensation from their employing brokers for activities that require a license.

139. 2. The affiliate broker is responsible for complying with proper procedure, which includes: filling out TREC Form 1, obtaining the releasing and accepting brokers' signatures, paying the fees, relocating his or her license, seeing that the license is posted on the new broker's office wall, and notifying the real estate commission. The releasing broker's responsibility is terminated upon signing the release form and retaining a copy.

140. 1. An affiliate broker may be licensed with only one broker.

141. 4. The affiliate broker acted improperly. An affiliate broker may collect a fee only from his employing broker. He should have turned the bonus check over to the employing broker. The broker could then pay the affiliate broker his share of the bonus or passed all of it to him, in accordance with the company policy.

142. 4. Affiliate brokers may only do what their employing broker empowers them to do. In this instance, the broker's license is suspended and the broker may not authorize any one of his or her staff to conduct broker activities. The licensees need to return their licenses to the commission or seek the commission's permission to transfer to another firm within ten days of the broker's suspension, or be subject to suspension of their licenses as well.

143. 3. Each office must be under the direction of a licensed real estate broker licensed at that address. Brokers can have branch offices, but each office must be under the direction of a licensed real estate broker licensed at that address. No broker may have more than one license in effect at a time.

144. 4. The affiliate broker must send the TREC Form 1 signed by both brokers along with the appropriate fee. The releasing broker is released from any further responsibilities upon signing the release form. The releasing broker needs to retain a copy of the form to show the license was released on the date specified on TREC Form 1.

145. 2. The notice must be transmitted to the commission within ten days of the change of business location. The broker must submit verification (from the proper governmental authority) that the new address conforms to local zoning laws and ordinances. The existing licenses remain in effect and do not specify the address of the firm. The commission, upon receipt of the change of address, will make the appropriate address changes of all other licensees licensed with the firm.

146. 3. The broker may not offer a title opinion, which could be construed as an unauthorized practice of law. Further, the broker is not responsible for the accuracy of the closing statement if provided by an attorney or title company; and state law requires that copies of all documents involved in the transaction be retained for three years.

147. 1. Producing a full-price offer that meets the terms of the listing agreement to the seller from a ready, willing, and able buyer constitutes the earning of a commission even if the seller rejects the offer, because the broker accomplished the job he or she was hired to do. The purchaser, at this point, has no contract with the seller and the seller may reject the offer. Simply having a listing agreement does not ensure a commission. A selling broker may not have a listing contract.

148. 2. State law permits brokers to keep only an amount sufficient to keep the account open when all other funds have been disbursed. The broker may not make periodic withdrawals of those funds used to keep the account open.

149. 2. State law requires that brokers keep transaction records for at least three years.

150. 3. An affiliate broker may not accept a fee from anyone other than his or her employing broker. Additionally, such fees must be disclosed to all parties to the transaction. A fee in return for a referral may be construed as an illegal kickback, which is a violation of RESPA.

151. 4. The broker may say "thank you" to the airline pilot, but may not pay him any money. A broker may pay a referral fee only to another licensed broker.

152. 2. The real estate commission must be notified within 60 days of conviction. Both the conviction and the broker's failure to notify the real estate commission within 60 days violated commission regulations. If a hearing had been requested within the 60-day period, the commission could have considered possible alternative action to take in this case.

153. 4. The applicant must also meet other requirements. He or she must also be at least 18 years of age, have a high school diploma or GED certificate, reside in the state for at least 45 days, be sponsored by a licensed broker and have no past criminal record (other than driving offenses), without first submitting a request for a hearing before the commission.

154. 4. The new buyer does not have the right to cancel a signed contract in this situation. A purchaser of time-shares has a period of time in which he or she may rescind the contract. The amount of time depends on whether he or she had an actual inspection of the property.

155. 4. Commissions are always negotiable between the principal or customer and the agent. The commissions are not determined by law, the real estate commission, or by a group of local brokers.

156. 2. The broker may deposit this buyer's funds into an escrow account containing money from other customers and clients. Detailed record keeping is required. Monies may not be held in an unsecured place, such as a listing folder, or in the company operating account.

157. 2. Affiliate brokers licensed as brokers on or after July 1, 2005, must complete 120 hours of post-license education within three years of license issuance, and thereafter have the same 16 hours requirement of affiliate brokers.

158. 3. The broker and the owner may renegotiate the lease any time that they both mutually agree to renegotiate.

159. 4. There is no standard fee, and all of the commissioners shall forfeit their licenses because the commission may not set fees or commissions charged by licensees. The amount of the commission charged is negotiated between the broker and the client or customer.

160. 1. A broker is required to maintain at least one escrow or trust account for deposit of any monies belonging to others which may come into his or her possession. The broker must submit proof of such account upon initial firm license application and upon each renewal of license thereafter.

161. 2. An adequate description, such as the property address, is required, but not the legal description. The listing agreement must include a fair housing statement. Listings must have an asking price and a definable broker fee to avoid an unintentional prohibited net listing. Listings must have a definite termination date.

162. 4. Tennessee is a trust deed state. There is no redemption time after a foreclosure. The borrower/owner has waived any statutory right of redemption in the language of the trust deed.

163. 2. Retired licensees may not perform any act requiring a license until after the license has been made active, which includes obtaining errors and omissions insurance. Commission rates or fees are required to avoid net listings. The state law does not address the issue of whether or not to include a broker protection clause.

164. 2. As of January 1, 1996, the listing or selling brokerage firm may act as a facilitator or transactional broker. As a transactional broker, there is no requirement to default to a form of agency.

165. 4. The listing company is obligated to use its best efforts to sell the property, but is not obligated to buy the property if no one else does. Any ads should be placed in publications likely to reach an appropriate buyer, and this does not necessarily mean statewide coverage.

166. 3. As of July 1, 2005, licenses issued will normally be issued for a two year period. However, E&O insurance will continue to be issued on a prorated fee to expire on December 31 of each even-numbered year.

167. 2. The broker's fee is earned when he/she produces the ready, willing, and able buyer's offer—in this case, May 1. It is common for the listing agreement with the seller to agree to wait until the closing date for payment but is not a requirement. The broker's fee is not dependent upon the closing date or the recording date; deeds are not always recorded, and ownership transfers when the deed is voluntarily delivered and accepted.

168. 3. The attorney, broker, or title company conducting the closing is responsible for calculating the prorations, searching the title, providing the buyers and sellers with copies of closing settlement sheets, and preparing the deed. If the broker is conducting the closing, he or she may not prepare the deed nor is he or she qualified to render an opinion of title. If an affiliate broker conducts the closing, it must be under the direct supervision of the broker, and the broker remains responsible for the conduct of the closing.

169. 4. A broker or affiliate broker may not render an opinion of title without possible charges of practicing law without a license. A broker or affiliate broker may maintain time schedules, provide net data, anticipate decision-making alternatives, coordinate inspections, and deliver some documents and escrow monies to the closing attorney.

170. 4. The broker may conduct the closing as closings are within the scope of the duties of a real estate broker. The broker may not prepare the deed or conduct the title search. An attorney-at-law and a title company may conduct the closing. An attorney-in-fact is not a lawyer.

171. 4. The aggrieved party has the right to up to a $15,000 maximum recovery from the real estate education and recovery account. The licensee's license may be suspended or revoked until the amount is paid back in full plus interest at the effective rate set by law.

172. 2. The purpose of the Tennessee Real Estate Education and Recovery Account is to provide a means of compensation for actual monetary losses suffered by individuals as a result of the acts of a licensee in violating the license law or committing other illegal acts related to a real estate transaction.

173. 3. The maximum compensation that will be paid from the Tennessee Real Estate Education and Recovery Account for any single transaction is $15,000.

174. 3. The maximum that can be paid on any one transaction is $15,000. If the total amount paid out against a licensee reaches $30,000 the liability of the account is terminated. The purpose of the fund is to provide a means of compensation for actual monetary losses suffered by individuals as a result of the acts of a licensee in violating the license law or committing other illegal acts related to a real estate transaction.

175. 2. The licensee must repay the full amount plus interest to the account in order to have his or her license reinstated.

176. 2. The minimum balance of $500,000 must be maintained in the Tennessee Real Estate Education and Recovery Account.

177. 1. The licensee's license may be suspended or revoked, at the discretion of the commission. The suspension or revocation is not automatic.

178. 4. All affiliate brokers and brokers are required to have E&O insurance. It is optional for the firm.

179. 1. The errors and omissions insurance must be continuous from the date of the event up to and including the date the lawsuit is filed. Thus, the affiliate is not covered for this event because his insurance lapsed and will not cover past events since the insurance was not continuous. Because he let his insurance lapse, E&O will not cover past claims unless they were filed against him during the insured and licensed period.

180. 4. No E&O insurance is required for those who place their licenses in temporary retirement. Note that these licensees may not conduct any real estate business while in "retirement."

181. 1. If the commission is unable to obtain errors and omissions insurance to insure all licensees who chose to participate in the insurance program at a reasonable premium, the requirement of insurance coverage is void during that period. The commission rules make no distinction between independent and franchised real estate companies for insurance purposes.

182. 4. The company cannot refuse to represent Broker Z if he does not agree to settle out of court, but is only required to pay a claim up to the amount that they were willing to settle for out of court. Any amount over that will be at Broker Z's expense. Broker Z should not cancel his insurance.

183. 2. The listing agent has a duty to inquire of the seller and inform the buyer, their agents, or facilitators showing the property about this latent defect. A latent defect is one that is known by the seller and not the buyer and would not be discovered by an ordinary inspection of the property.

184. 4. Affiliate Broker K may show the buyer the property and treat him as a customer. Since K represents the broker of XYZ Realty, he is serving as a seller's agent regardless of who listed the property. A dual agent is an agent of both. Without the informed consent of the seller and buyer, K cannot serve as a dual agent. Unless specifically designated by the broker, K cannot serve as a designated agent.

185. 4. K may not tell her seller that the buyer was willing to pay full price. Any information received from a customer prior to notifying the customer that K represented the seller must remain confidential. K may write up the buyer customer's offer and must promptly present it to the seller.

186. 4. The affiliate broker K must first execute a bilateral agency agreement with this buyer to establish the buyer agency relationship. Tennessee law requires a bilateral written agreement, signed by both the buyer and the agent, to establish any form of real estate agency or subagency. The signing of an agency disclosure form can never establish the agency relationship.

187. 1. The company has no new listings. Tennessee license law states that agency or subagency relationships cannot be created without a bilateral written agency agreement. There was no subagency established between the broker and J; therefore J was not authorized to represent the company in obtaining listings for them. J was misrepresenting his status to sellers. J was not a subagent of the firm. The broker has no new listings as a result of J's efforts and has violated the license laws. The broker violated Tennessee license law.

188. 4. A facilitator represents neither the buyer nor the seller in a specific transaction. A facilitator simply brokers the transaction without becoming the advocate of either party. Since the licensee does not represent the seller or the buyer, no agency status has been created.

189. 2. The broker's company establishes a bilateral single agency agreement to serve as a buyer's agent with its buyer clients. The broker and all subagents in the company work for the buyer's best interest.

190. 4. Verbal notification that the broker will be the buyer's agent cannot establish an agency relationship of representation in Tennessee. Representation is determined by written agreement, not by who pays the real estate commission. The broker misrepresented himself because the broker had no written agreement to serve as an agent of anyone.

191. 3. The broker misrepresented himself and his company. The broker, in taking an agency listing on the dental office, established an agency relationship with the seller. The broker and his company represent the seller. The buyer is not represented. The broker cannot represent one party and serve as a facilitator to another in the same transaction.

192. 4. The broker did not violate the license laws, rules, or regulations and should not be punished. The law does not require the buyer or the broker to enter into an agency agreement. If agency is to be established, it must be a two-sided agreement. If the broker does not want to agree to an agency agreement, there is no need to offer it. If the buyer wants representation, he may seek it elsewhere.

193. 4. The firm cannot obtain written permission from both parties to serve as the agent of each client on the same transaction. Written permission from both clients to default to dual agency, designated agency, and facilitator status are alternative methods of compliance with Tennessee laws of agency/non-agency.

194. 1. Tennessee does not recognize community property rights. Tennessee does, however, recognize tenancy by the entireties, tenancy in severalty, joint tenancy and tenancy in common. Community property rights pertain to ownership rights in those states which are governed by the Spanish influence. Louisiana has the French influence and most other states, including Tennessee, use the English influence with some modifications.

195. 4. Tennessee recognizes both conventional life estates and life estates pur autre vie. Tennessee has not recognized curtesy and dower since 1977, so it does not have legal life estates as a result of the death of a spouse. Tennessee is not a community property state.

196. 2. The transfer tax is determined by the Tennessee Legislature.

197. 2. Property tax amounts and due dates vary in every city and county in the state.

198. 4. The client or other party to whom a licensee provides services as an agent, subagent, or facilitator shall not be liable for damages for the misrepresentations of the licensee unless the client or party knew or had reason to know of the misrepresentations.